Figure 1 LEE CUMMINGS THE AUTHOR

(THE NEGRO QUESTION: PART 2

Copyright © 2013 by (LEE BERNARD CUMMINGS)

ISBN:978-1492719120

TABLE OF CONTENTS

THE STOCKING OF EUROPEAN COLONIES

Figure 2EMANUEL BOWENS MAP OF AFRICA DATED 1747

When the European powers carved up Africa it was the custom of the European kings in those days to send out a cartographer (map maker) to outline and pinpoint his holdings. There was a cartographer in 1747 who went by the name of Emanuel Bowen, this man held **the title of royal Cartographer** for two European kings, King George 2nd of England and king Louis xv of France.

4

What is unusual about the map that Emanuel Bowen brought back to these two kings is that in the center of the map Bowen shows that **the true name of the so called slave coast was none other than the Kingdom of Judah!** Judah was known by four different names at that time, Judah Whidah,Quidah or Abier. What does this mean to those of us who have been in hot pursuit of the truth? It means that we have the proof from the royal mapmaker himself that Judah was indeed listed among the inhabitants of Africa. Of even greater interest is the fact that the maps were not disputed by the two kings! You would do well to take heed to the fact that the British laid claim to the so called slave coast and that its inhabitants were sold into the British colonies and one being in North America. How authentic is this map?

NORTHWESTERN UNIVERSITY
AUTHENTIC MAP OF WEST AFRICA

The University of Northwestern (Evanston Illinois) has this map in their inventory and lists it as an authentic map of West Africa, 1747 by Emanuel Bowen. Even to this day there is a fort there called **the fort of Ajudah.** If you pull up the information on line or at Northwestern University this is what you will see.

Northwestern university library maps of Africa
Title: **A new and accurate map of negroland**
Cartographer:Emanuel Bowen 1747
Size of Image;35x43 CM.
Place of publication: **London**
Subject: **West Africa**
Identification: Northwestern University Library

A CULTURAL HISTORY OF ATLANTIC WORLD
JOHN K. THORNTON
BOSTON UNIVERSITY
CAMBRIDGE UNIVERSITY PRESS

On pages 64 and 70 reference is made that the French had a director at Whydah (Judah) and that the French also had a trading post at Savi, the capital of (Whydah) Judah! Did the writer know that the name Whydah was Judah? I don't know but one thing is for certain, the Europeans seem to know where the Negro in the Americas' and the Caribbean came from!

LOUISIANA STATE UNIVERSITY
THE SHIPS THAT CAME FROM JUDAH

There is a publication written at Louisiana state University
   Titled: Creole New Orleans
   Race and Americanization
   Edited by R. Hirsch and Joseph Logsdon
   Louisiana State University Press
   Baton Rouge and London

On page 67 of this publication are the notes of a white slaver recalling the inventory of human beings on a cargo ship…..lets' see what he writes. He writes that " sixteen slave trading ships arrived from the Senegal region. **Six ships came from Juda** and landed at the mouth of the Mississipi and in 1731 one ship form **juda** landed 464 slaves at the mouth of the Mississipi. **On page 69** it states that "**the company of India had a trading post at Juda** (Gulf of Benin) there it competed with all the nations of Europe! The **Portuguese was taking the upper hand at Juda**! Northwestern university, Boston University and Louisiana state University have in its possession documents calling the slave coast of Africa Juda. If you won't believe me surely you will believe academia aren't they supposed to be the caretakers of the truth? You also have a town named Ajuda that was in existence before the Portuguese ever

Figure 3 THE PORT TOWN AJUDA, SO NAMED BEFORE THE ARRIVAL OF THE EUROPEAN

set foot on West African soil. The Kingdom of Judah (slave coast) was controlled by the British and all of these black Jews came pouring in to the British colonies. The question that arises from the research is how did these black Jews get to west

Africa and when did they begin to arrive? The answer is hidden with Abraham of the Bible....lets visit Abraham!

CHAPT 2: O ABRAHAM HOW COULD THIS BE?

Figure 4 MARI PAINTING SCENE

This is a painting that was found in Ancient Mesopotamia, it is

called the Mari painting scene. The brown skinned people in

the picture are the ancient Sumerians. Sumer (Shinar in your

Bible) was located near the Tigris and Euphrates river, modern day Iran and Iraq. The Bible (Genesis 11:31) records that Abraham had his origination in Ur of the Chaldees. Ancient Ur was in the land of Sumer (Shinar in your Bible) or Mesopotamia. Of particular interest is the tablets that were found in Sumer in which the Ancient Sumerians describe themselves as the black headed people. One of the mighty men that lived in that generation that went by the name of Sargon the great stated in his writings that he ruled over the black headed people. See the Negro Question Part 1 pages 7 & 8.

Priest Guiding a Sacrificial Bull - Fragment of a mural painting from the palace of Zimri-Lim, Mari (modern Tell Hariri, Iraq). 2040-1870 B.C.

Figure 5 BLACK MAN OF SUMER UR

From the evidence cited above ,the image of the ancient Sumerians, the statement from the Sumerians describing

9

themselves as black and the statement from Sargon the great

one must conclude that the ancient people of Sumer or Ur were

black people, making Abraham of the Bible a black man! I

have located a picture of a few warriors from Mesopotamia

(Sumer or Ur) that called themselves' the Elamites. Take a

close look at these guys because they were and are most

certainly black, see next page.

ELAMITE WARRIOR

For a further reference see Genesis the tenth chapter and verse
22. It clearly states that Elam is the son of Shem, Abrahams father.

Figure 6 KING SHULGI, SUMERIAN KING OF UR.

Figure 7 KING GUDEA OF LAGASH

Figure 8 SARGON THE GREAT OF SUMER

The portrait that you saw on page 11 is of Sargon the Great, it is said of this black king that he ruled from Elam to the Mediterranean. This guy was from the same region that Abraham was from and basically what is evolving from the introduction to this book is that brother Abraham was indeed a black man and Sarah his sister was a black woman, fact not fiction! From this point of view I will attempt to trace the footsteps of Abrahams' sons, Israel and Esau. For the record I am not interested in race, I am only interested in one thing and what might that be? That the people of God (the so called Negro) wake up from this deep sleep that we are in and recognize that we are indeed the people of the bible.

CHAPTER 3: THE FOOTSTEPS OF THE BLACK SEED OF ABRAHAM

In order to trace the seed of Abraham I will have to use the Bible as a reference. What is that big book sitting on Grannies' table? The bible is a history book of the creation and restoration of the earth after the war in heaven. The Bible is also the history of the world before it happens (the foreknowledge of God) and lastly the Bible is a record of the genealogy of the children of Israel without which Israel could never find himself! Lets' turn to the book of Chronicles in the King James Version of the Bible. In 1st Chronicles, the first chapter, verse 34 it reads" and **Abraham begat Isaac and the sons of Isaac; Esau and Israel**. The son that we will use for the purpose of this book will be Israel. If you are a bible reader you already know that Israel original name was Jacob. This is the lineage (sons of Israel) of Israel. In 1st Chronicles Chapter two and verses one and it reads, these are the sons of Israel; Reuben, Simeon, Levi, Judah, Issachar, Zebulun, Dan, Joseph, Benjamin, Naphtali, Gad and Asher. The book of Exodus, chapter one and verses 1-5 reads; Now these are the names of the children of Israel, which came into Egypt; every man and his household came with (Jacob) Israel; Reuben, Simeon, Levi, Judah, Issachar, Zebulun, Benjamin, Dan, Naphtali, Gad, Asher and Joseph. All of the souls that came out of Israel were seventy souls: for Joseph was in Egypt already. Now the word Egypt means black and in order for me to write this book effectively I must show you pictures of the true Egyptian. Why? Because we have some people in Egypt today who are pawning themselves off to the world as the true Egyptians. The people in Egypt today are not Egyptians, they are Turks left over from the old Turkish Empire! See image on next page of an ancient Egyptian.

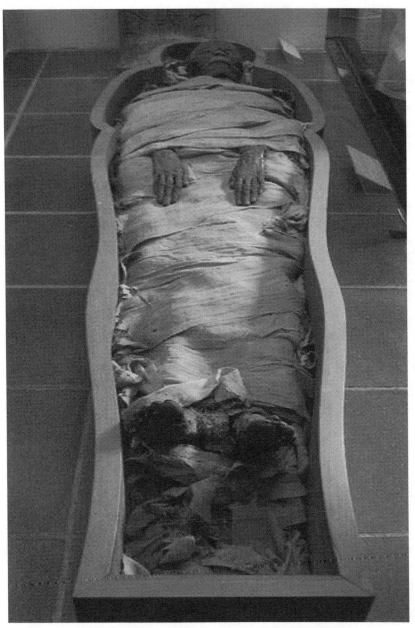

Figure 9 Black Egyptian mummy housed at Vatican Museum

If you won't believe me I know you will believe the Catholic Church, the Vatican church knows what a true Egyptian looks like that's why they have one housed on display at the Vatican.

Figure 10 EGYPTIAN QUEEN NEFATERI

Figure 11 LAST ETHNIC EGYPTIAN PRESIDENT ANWAR SADAAT

The Europeans know that the ancient Egyptians were black why else would National Geographic do a front cover piece called, the Black Pharaohs of Egypt? The problem with this generation (and there are many) is that there is a major failure to read books. If you would force yourself to read you will know that **all the peoples of the world (all races) have been migrating for the last 6000 years.** In fact the proof is in the black community, we are a people that was removed out of our land in 1619 and brought to the Americas' and the Caribbean's' as (captives) prisoners of war and we have been here ever since! The European barbarians came out of the Caucus Mountains in the 5th century A.D and sacked the Roman Empire and begin to dwell in old Roman territories. The barbarian Angles, Jutes and Saxons (modern day Britain) migrated to the British Isles, they did not originate there, this is a historical fact! Now that I have established that the ancient Egyptians were a black people lets' run to Genesis and see if the seed of Israel had lost its blackness. In the 50th chapter of Genesis verses 1 and 2 we see that Jacob Israel died. in verse 7 it says" Joseph went up to bury his father; and

16

with him went up all the servants of Pharaoh, the elders of his house and all the elders of the land of Egypt. Verse 8 and all the house of Joseph and his brothers and his father's house; verse 10 and they came to the threshing floor of Atad, which is beyond Jordan, and there they mourned with a great and very sore lamentation. Verse 11 and when the inhabitants of the land, the Canaanites saw the mourning in the floor of Atad , they said, this is a grievous mourning to the Egyptians! What is the point? The Canaanites could not tell the difference between the black Egyptians and the black Israelites because they both had black skin. Is their further proof? Yes there was a coin found in the Cairo museum with the image of Joseph on it he was depicted as a black man. See the image of Joseph on next page.

Figure 12 Joseph in Egypt

This image of Joseph was found on some coins in the Museum in Cairo Egypt with Josephs name and inscription, Joseph Viceroy of Egypt. In case you don't know it, this is the Joseph of the Bible. The Europeans depict or paint Joseph as a white man but the ancient Egyptians depicted the Hebrew captives as black people. You can pull this image up on the internet by pulling up the; Joseph coin found, article Al Ahram News, Cairo Egypt.

CHAPT 4   THE ASSYRIAN INVASION OF ISRAEL

KING JEHU & THE PRINCES OF ISRAEL

The **"Black Obelisk"** of Shalmaneser III (reigned 858-824 B.C.)
Is a black limestone bas-relief sculpture from Nimrud (ancient Kalhu),
in northern Iraq. It is currently displayed in the British Museum.
It is the most complete Assyrian obelisk yet discovered, and is historically
significant because it displays the earliest ancient depiction of an Israelite.
It was erected in Assyria as a public monument in 825 B.C. which was
during a time of civil war. The Obelisk was discovered by archaeologist
Sir Henry Layard in 1846. The obelisk features twenty reliefs,
five on each side. They depict five different subdued kings, bringing tribute
and prostrating before the Assyrian king Shalmaneser III.

I have enlarged the images off of Shalmanesers' Obelisk to give you an idea of how the Assyrian captors depicted the ancient Hebrew Israelites of the bible. You will need to take careful notice that not only are these brothers depicted as black men but they also have napy afros! Below is an image of King Jehu of Israel kneeling before Shalmaneser which dosen't give a good detail of his afro or his blackness but on the next page you will see that the Hebrew Israelites in the procession are were black indeed

King Jehu of Israel, leads a procession bringing tribute to Assyrian King Shalmaneser - 853

King Jehu of Israel, leads a procession bringing tribute to Assyrian King Shalmaneser - 853 B.C. #4

Figure 13 Black Hebrew Israelites with nappy hair like lambs wool and fringes on the bottom of their garments.

See also numbers 15: 37-41 Israel was to put fringes on the border of their garments to remember the commandments of the God of Israel.

Figure10 This is an Enlarged Image of the 1ˢᵗ Black Hebrew Israelite on page 19, Shalmanaser the 3rd black obelisk, most likely a prince in Israel.

Figure 14 This is an enlarged image of the 3rd Hebrew Israelite male on page 19, Shalmanaser 3rd black obelisk, most likely a prince in Israel.

SENNACHERIBS HEXAGONAL PRISM

**Figure 15 THIS PRISM RECORDS THE REIGN OF
SENNACHERIB 689 B.C**

I am not going to write everything that was found on this Prism (Time Capsul) but I will reveal the treasure that has been saved here. The prism states that **Sennacherib took captive Hezekiahs** harem, daughters, **male and female musicians** back to Ninevah my royal city. For you bible scholars out there the musicians came from the tribe of Levi and on the next page I have provided for you what a hebrew Israelite looked like before the so called European Renaisance period.

23

SIEGE OF LACHISH ASSYRIA CAN BE FOUND BRITISH & FRENCH MUSEUM 2 KINGS 18:14

`Figure 16 IMAGE OF CORN ROLLED HEBREWS

GOING INTO ASSYRIAN CAPTIVITY.

This image of the black Hebrew Israelites going into the Assyrian captivity is unmistakable. They are depicted as being black men with corn rolls and nappy braided facial hair and in order to emphasize this more perfectly I enlarged the image for you on the next page.

Figure 17 Enlarged image from page 23 of a black Hebrew Israelite male with corn rolls going into the Assyrian captivity.

Figure 18 This is an image of the black Hebrew Levite musicians that Sennacherib boasted on his Prism (Time Capsule) that he took captive back to Assyria. Sennacherib stated that he took the male and female musicians.

In the 15the chapter of 1st Chronicles (1st Chronicles 15:16-17,19,20 & 21) Verse 16 And **David spoke to the chief of the Levites to appoint their brethren to be the singers with instruments of music, Psalteries and Harps and Cymbals,** sounding by lifting up the voice with joy. Verse17 **so the singers, Heman Asaph and Ethan were appointed to sound with cymbals of brass. Verse 20 and Zechariah with Psalteries. Verse 21 And Mattithiah with Harps.** See 1ST Chronicles 25: 1-6 for clarification. Open your eyes, can't you see that these black Levite musicians indeed have in their hands the cymbals of brass, the Psalteries and the Harp? I am going to slow the image down for you by breaking the image in two so you can see the vision.

Top image: corn rolled Hebrew Israelite musicians: Asaph, Heman and Ethan with cymbals of brass and fringes on their robes.

Figure 19 Bottom Image: Corn rolled Hebrew Israelite Levite musicians Zachariah with the Psalteries, Matithiah with the Harp &fringes on bottom of their garments.

On the next page I am going to bring this image to a complete stop so that you can see the blackness of these Levite priests. It is unmistakable that these Levite priests are black men.

Figure 20 THE IMAGE OF THE HEBREW ISRAELITE MUSICIANS BLOWN UP FROM PAGES 26 & 27.

NAPHTALI ISRAEL GOING INTO ASSYRIAN

CAPTIVITY

With their belongings slung over their shoulders, Hebrew captives are being driven out of Astartu or Ashtaroth, by Assyrian warriors. Relief from Nimrud, time of Tiglath-Pileser III, 8th century B.C.

This scene is recorded in your bible in 2nd Kings 15:29 where

it reads; In the days of Pekah King of Israel came Tiglath pileser

King of Assyria and took all the land of **Naphtali** and carried them

captive to the land of Assyria.

Blown up image of Assyrian relief from Nimrud, time

of Tiglath Pileser 3rd. this image was taken from page 28 and

enlarged to show you the nappy hair and the blackness of

Israel. It is interesting that the Assyrians depicted the Hebrews as black people.

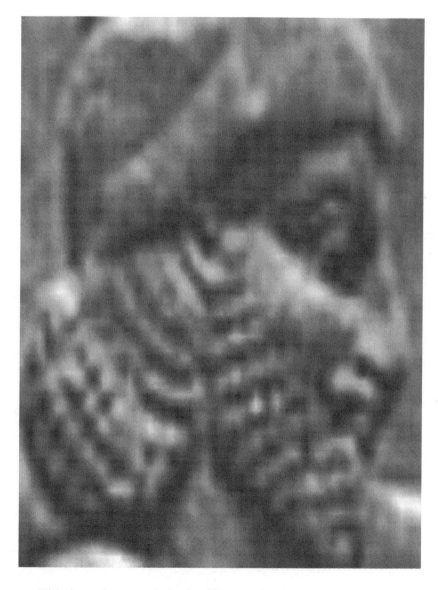

This is an image of Naphtali Israel from pages 29 & 30,

I enlarged the first Hebrew Israelite which is the 2nd black male from left to right. You can see clearly that the Naphtali Israel is depicted as a black man with nappy hair and nappy facial hair.

ASSYRIANS INVASION OF LACHISH

Assyrian relief: After the conquest of the Judean city of Lachish: king Sennacherib sits on his throne, as the ruler of Lachish stands before him, and the citizens bow down to him.

Figure 21 ASSYRIAN RELIEF BRITISH MUSEUM: BLACK HEBREWS WITH BRAIDS! See 2nd Chronicles 32: Verses 1 & 9.

This is an image of nappy headed (Braided hair) Israelites kneeling before the Assyrian King Sennacherib but notice the braided hair of the Judeans and the braided locks of the Judean ruler of Lachish. See the blown up images on the next page.

What further proof do we need?

Figure 22 This is a blown up image of one of the black Jews of Lachish
from page   31. The image is of the fourth man from left to right. He is a
black Judean male with an afro and a nappy beard, go to the next page and I
will illustrate this more perfectly. On the next page I will slow the image
down further to highlight the blackness of these citizens of Lachish.

When I enlarge the image from page 32 further you can see that this Hebrew Israelite Judean is a black man with a afro and nappy facial hair. The images don't lie, it is this modern historian who has been found out to be a liar. These guys are printing lies and the biggest liar in the United States is

Hollywood and the History channel! When the Assyrians would invade the land of Israel the Hebrew Israelites would flee into Libya (Africa) or further proof that what I write and say is not a lie you must turn to the 2nd chapter of Acts in your Bible and read what Peter says about the Israelites that came up to Jerusalem on the day of Pentecost. Peter is very explicit on where these Israelites dwelt, Acts 2:1,5,8 verse 8 and how hear we every man in our own tongue **wherein we were born** verse 10 Phrygian and Pamphylia in **Egypt** and in parts of **Libya about Cyrene.** The Apostle Peter is stating right here in the book of Acts that some of the Jews present in Jerusalem on the day of Pentecost were born in Libya (Africa) so how can I dispute that? In fact Acts the 13th chapter and verse one supports Peters' allegation. See Acts 13:1 now there were in the church that was at Antioch certain prophets and teachers: as Barnabas and Simeon that was **Niger** and Lucius of **Cyrene.** This place Cyrene was in Libya (upper Libya) or what you have come to know in this generation as Africa. Where did the name Africa come from? Black Hannibal was defeated by the Roman general Scipio Africanus at the battle of Carthage in

201 B.C and after the defeat at the hands of the Romans, this

mans name began to replace the name of Libya.

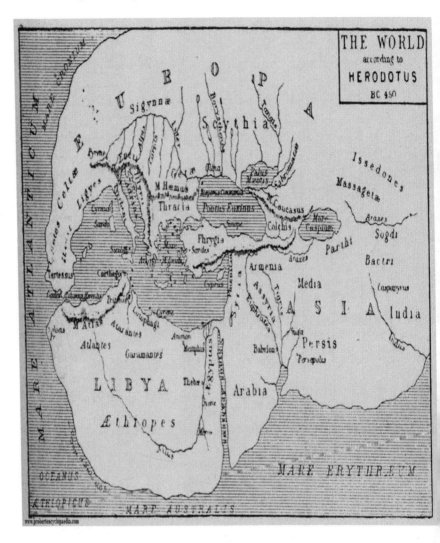

This would mean that the black man in America is

neither African nor American so then what are you? If you take

a very close look at this map you will see that lower Libya is

below the Sahara desert close to Ethiopia (Aethiopia) upper

Libya was what Peter called Cyrene. You can find that conversation in the 2nd chapter of Acts. All of the land below Libya lower is where Judah fled!

CHAPTER 5: THE BABYLONIAN INVASION OF JUDAH   609-586 B.C

The Babylonians came in contact with Judah around 609 B.C according to the Bible ((2nd Kings 24:1-3) but didn't invade the country until 606 B.C. How am I sure of this? The prophet Jeremiah stated that the Babylonian captivity would last 70 years (Jeremiah 25:1-12) and history states that the Babylonian captivity ended with the rise of Cyrus (Medo Persia) the great in 539 B.C. Now that you have the exact date that Cyrus began to reign, you subtract 539-609 and you get 70 years. The bible itself contains a passage of scripture that tells the world where the Hebrews fled to on the arrival of Nebuchadnezzar and his Chaldean army. See Jeremiah 43:1-7 verse 6, even men and women and children and the kings daughters and every person that Nebuzaradan the captain of the guard had left with Gedaliah the son of Ahikam the son of Shaphan and **Jeremiah the prophet** and Baruch the son of Neriah. Verse 7 So they came into the land of Egypt. For your own understanding you need to read the 42nd, 43rd and 44th chapter of Jeremiah. Jeremiah 44:1 The word that came to Jeremiah concerning all the Jews which dwell in the land of

Egypt (Africa)…at Taphanes…which dwell at Pathros. It is of extreme importance that you make a note that the Judeans fled into Egypt (Africa) taking Jeremiah the prophet and the seed of David with them for fear of Nebuchadnezzar. In case you didn't know it Egypt is in Africa (Libya) and so is Pathros. See Isiah the 11th chapter verse 11 And it shall come to pass in that day that the Lord shall set his hand again the second time to recover the remnant of his people which shall be left from Assyria, Egypt, Pathros, Cush, Ethiopia, Shinar(Sumer) and Hamath. All of these nations that the Lord says he is going to gather Israel from is in Africa (Libya) and are black people!

70 A.D ROMANS DESTROY JERUSALEM

**Figure 23 The arch of Titus Caesar depicting the Roman soldiers
looting the Temple in Jerusalem 70 A.D**

This image portrays the Roman soldiers stealing all of the
temple worship items out of the temple in Jerusalem in the year 70
A.D. Since you bought this book I will leave you with a gem. The
Roman soldiers walked away with something more precious than
gold and silver. When the Romans looted the temple in Jerusalem
they also took the birth records of Jesus (Yshw) Christ. Can I prove
this? Yes! The Levites used to keep all of records of the nation of
Judah, birth, death, land and marriage in the temple. In the book of
Luke (Luke 2:1-16) it has been recorded that Augustus Caesar took a
Census when Jesus was born. Augustus took a census in 28B.C,
8B.C and 14 A.D. In the entrance to Augustus Caesars' tomb is a
plaque called the deeds of Augustus Caesar. This Plaque gives the
proof that he took three Lustrums' (Census). Now Jesus (Yshw) was
born in Bethlehem, in the year 6 B.C, I know this is because Herod
murdered all the black Judean male babies from two years old and
younger. It has been recorded historically that Herod died in 4B.C,

39

do the math, 6-4=2. Augustus Caesar took three lustrums' (census) in his life time but there are only two that have anything to do with the Jesus (Yshw) of the Bible. If the Romans missed recording Jesus birth in 6 B.C then surely they would have recorded his existence in 14 A.D. In 14 A.D Jesus would have been 18 years old! All of the birth certificates of the New Testament characters would have been among the documents stolen by the Romans. You can find a detailed explanation of Jesus birth certificate in the book that I wrote, **The Jesus Mary Conspiracy page 49, the author Lee Cummings**. All of my books can be found on Amazon.com. So then the most precious thing that the Romans took out of the temple in 70 A.D was the birth certificate of Jesus Christ not the gold and silver. The birth certificate of Jesus Christ is sitting in the Vatican vault to this day! Vespasian Caesar had a coin minted a year later to commemorate the event.

Figure 24 This is a coin minted by Vespasian Caesar in 71 A.D commemorating his victory over Judah.

See the back side of the coin blown up on next page.

IMAGE ON BACK OF COIN MINTED BY VESPASIAN CAESAR

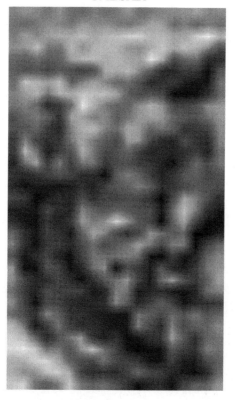

Figure 25 IS THIS SIMON BAR GIORA ISRAEL 70 A.D?

This image is of a black Judean on the back of the coin minted by Vespasian Caesar on page 38. Although the resolution is horrible it's the best that I could do, so we have to work with it. This Judean is shown to have black hair, black skin, black nose and big black lips. I know from the writings of Josephus the Hebrew Israelite Historian that one Simon Bar Giora was a Judean rebel leader captured alive by Vespasian Caesar and brought back to Rome where he and the other Hebrews were paraded before the Roman people. History records that this Simon Bar Giora Israel was lashed and then either choked to death or beheaded.

I am of the opinion that this is Simon Giora Israel because all the other rebel Judean leaders had been killed while trying to fend off the Roman invasion of Jerusalem in 70A.D. Simon Bar Giora Israel and the other Hebrew captives were brought to Rome to be sported in front of the Roman people. If anybody knew what an Hebrew Israelite looked like it would be the Egyptians, Assyrians and the Romans. Each one of these conquering Empires painted the Hebrew Israelite of the Bible as black people. When the Romans invaded Jerusalem in 70 A.D the black Hebrew Israelites had only one escape route and that was South into Libya (Africa). They followed the Nile River down into West Africa. I have found it interesting that all of the black nations (Egypt & Assyria) and empires that led Israel away as a captive recorded them as black people, with braids, afros and corn rolled hair. The white captors; the British, French, Portuguese, Dutch, Spanish and (Catholic Church) tried to paint the Hebrews white. If it had not been for the internet these images that I have been blessed to share with you would have been practically impossible to find.

CHAPTER 6: THE BLACK ARAB INVASION OF

JERUSALEM

Portrait of an Arab - Horace Vernet (1789-1863)

The true Arabs were always understood to be a black people, in fact the black Arabs were depicted as such up until the invasion of Arabia by the Ottoman Turk empire. This image was painted by Horace Vernet.

Arabs Crossing the Desert - Jean-Leon Gerome (1824-1904)

The black man Abraham had a son by the name of Ishmael who was Abrahams' first born. See Genesis chapter 16 verses 1-3 & verse 15. The bible tells you that the name of Abrahams' first son was Ishmael and Ishmael is the father of the true Arabs. The original Arabs were a black people just like their father Ishmael the son of Abraham. These are the true Arabs of

44

antiquity. The white Arab in the hood; your liquor store and gas station are imposters! This white Arab can't prove his lineage.

Arab Chieftain And His Entourage - Adolf Schreyer (1828-1899)

The lineage of the white Arab does not trace itself back to Abraham, they can only trace their lineage back to Japheth the son of Noah. This Japheth is the white European and they either know this or have been taught the same garbage that we have. On the next page there is an image that was painted by

Adolf Schreyer titled the pursuit where the Arabs of Arabia are still being represented as black people.

The Pursuit - Adolf Schreyer (1828-1899)

Figure 26 THE BLACK SONS OF ISHMAEL: THE ARABS OF YESTERDAY

The Arab Prince - Rudolph Ernst (1854-1932)

You can see based on the date listed at the bottom of this image that the timeline for the blackness of the Arabian has now shifted to the twentieth century. Ishmael (the true black Arabian) is being represented as a black man for at least 200

47

years beginning in the 18th century and ending in the 20th century. According to the ancient artifacts the original Arab was always a black nappy headed man.

BLACK ARAB WITH CORNROLLS!

Figure 27 STONE PANEL FROM NORTH PALACE OF ASHURBANIPAL 645 B.C

The sons of Ishmael have always been black and history hasn't forgotten them....we have! I have blown this image up

48

on the next page so you can get a detailed view of the blackness of the black Arab.

Figure 28 This is an image of an ancient Black Arab from 645 B.C

The images and the coins from antiquity don't lie people, it is the racist Historians that are lying.

Lantern slide, showing Persians posing. Photographed by Gen Sir Percy Molesworth Sykes - circa 1900

Thank God for technology (CAMERA) because this generation may never have known the truth. Who are these white Arabs in Arabia today and what happened? I will tell you what happened it is called the Ottoman Turk Empire.

50

THE OTTOMAN TURKS

Figure 29 SELIM 1
The Ottoman Turks Invaded Egypt , Syria, Palestine and all of
Arabia bringing them under Turkish control in 1517 A.D. In the years
of 1534 and 1535 he invaded and annexed Iran and Iraq. This is the
beginning of the whitening of Arabia.

This Selim 1 conquered all of what you have come to know as the middle east and then proceeded to migrate his Turkish subjects to that region of the world. The people that inhabited Arabia were black people until the coming of the Ottoman Turk Empire, this is a historical fact. The white Turks pushed the black Arabians (Abrahams' seed) out of Arabia and for some inexplicable reason they started to think that they really were the black people who they displaced! The Turk that is in Egypt has been brainwashed into thinking he is the descendant of the ancient Egyptians even though he looks nothing like the artifacts. This may be one of the reasons he keeps cutting off the noses of the Egyptian statues. This phenomenon (amnesia) has spread all over the region of the Middle East, these European Turks have deluded themselves into thinking that they are the original Arabs of history. So now we can put a date on the arrival of the white Arabs (1517) to Arabia. That is why the Lord had Daniel to write in the 7th chapter of Daniel (Daniel7:25) that the beast (Anti-Christ) would try to change times (History), laws and seasons. The black Arabians drove the black Jews out of Jerusalem in the year 640 A.D and again the only route that these fleeing Judeans could take was South, following the Nile river down into West Africa. These are the facts ladies and gentleman not that free education garbage that we receive in these so called schools of higher learning. The time for believing everything people tell you is over with, that is what children do. It is time for you to be weaned from the breast. The Lord had it written in Isaiah (Isaiah 28:9 & 10) whom shall he teach knowledge? Who shall he make to understand doctrine? Those that are weaned from milk and drawn from the breast. In the book of Corinthians, (1st Corinthians13:11) Paul writes, "when I was a child, I spoke as a child, I understood as a child, I thought as a child: but when I became a man, I put away childish things". What we have been taught in the Americas and the Caribbean are childish things, we really need grow past the foolishness of what we have been taught. What is wrong with you or me doing independent research outside of a Government sponsored education? The answer is in the Willie Lynch letters, this would produce a free man, woman and child! That's why Jesus said", you shall know the truth and the truth shall make you free. Chapter seven will deal with the black Jewish empires of Ghana, Mali and Songhai.

CHAPTER 7: BLACK JEWISH EMPIRES OF WEST AFRICA

GHANA 700-1235 A.D

You cannot bring up the discussion of the empire of Ghana without mentioning the great Bantu migration (60 million people) that took place in western, southern and eastern Africa from 300 A.D to 1500 A.D.

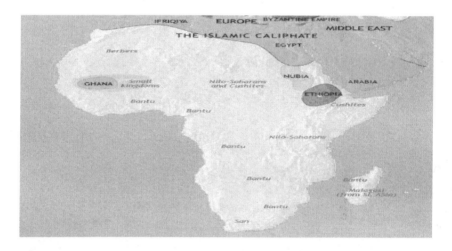

Bantu was once the language that was spoken from Ghana to South Africa. Bantu was spoken in Ghana, Ashanti (Levite), Lemba (Levite), Kingdom of Judah (slave coast), Congo and Zimbabwe! And so it was that 60 million Bantu (Hebrew Israelites) speaking people, over 1500 year period, flooded West Africa. Why would all of these people flee to west Africa? Some fled the Assyrian invasion of Israel in 722

B.C, some fled the Babylonian invasion of Israel in 606 B.C, some fled the Roman invasion of Israel in 70 A.D and some fled the black Arab invasion of Israel in 640 A.D! Is there any proof of this? Of course there is lets' examine the proof that is on the ground.

BANTU HEBREW NAMES

There is a town in the Congo called Kongolo, the prefix KON in Hebrew means settled in and the suffix GOLO means exile. Put the two Hebrew words together you get" settled in exile"! lets' look at the Bantu word <u>Bar Congo which means girded sons</u>. **In Hebrew, the word is spelled** <u>bar Khagore which means girded sons</u>, coincidence? Did you know that the world Guinea is derived from the world Ghana which means warrior King? Lets' look at a few more Bantu words, <u>lets look at the word son in Bantu, the word son is spelled</u> **Bena, Bana** and <u>in Hebrew the word is spelled</u> **Ben**. <u>The word</u> **water** <u>in Bantu is spelled</u> **Mayi** and <u>in Hebrew it is spelled</u> **Mayim**. The word thanks or praise in Bantu is spelled Tondo, Matondo, in Hebrew the word is spelled Tonda. In Bantu the word, to play, is spelled Tseka-Tsaka but in Hebrew the word, to play, is

54

spelled Tsakak! The Bantu word for God is Yah-abe and the Hebrew word for God is Yah. You don't have to be a rocket scientist to see that Bantu and Hebrew is the same language. As far as Ghana is concerned lets' hear the testimony of an author of the middle ages known as Edrisi (found in Hebrewisms of west Africa, page 234) he writes," speaking of Lamlam, whence slaves were dragged into captivity by the inhabitants of Ghana. Tacour states that there were only two towns in this district which he places to the south of the kingdom of Ghana and adds: according to what the people of this country report the inhabitants are Jews! Hadji el-Eghwaati, writing in 1242 adds this testimony, there is a race of people in Tuggurt called Medjehariah which occupy one separate quarter of the town. They were Jews in former time but <u>to escape death with which they were menace by the natives, they made profession of Islam</u>! Let me play the game of intrigue, were there any towns or rivers in the southern states where these Bantu speaking people were enslaved? According to the research done by Joseph E. Holloway (His book The African Heritage of American English) on page 107 he lists Bantu place names in nine Southern States. In **Alabama 28, Georgia18, Florida 31, Mississippi 14, North Carolina 26, South Carolina 104, and Virginia 26, Louisiana and Texas.** It appears that the language the white kidnappers forbade the Hebrew captives to speak was Bantu **(HEBREW)**. The name Ghana is not the name of a country, the name Ghana was the title that the king held. In the book, Hebrewisms of West Africa, Joseph J Williams writes that Za el Yemeni came to Kuka about 300 A.D an ancient abode of the Songhai tribe. He established a line of kings known as the ZA,Dja or the Dia dynasty. This founder of the the first Sudanic dynasty in western Africa was a black Jew. Za established his capital at Gao on the eastern upper Niger river. Concerning Islam in Ghana it is a known fact that Islam penetrated the Sudan but the the rulers of Ghana didn't accept Islam as one of their state religions. Gao, the capital of Ghana, was separated into two cities; the first one was the residence of the King. This city had a fortress and the second city contained twelve mosques in which the Mohammedan merchants could settle or wait until they transacted their business. This quote was taken from the book,

From Babylon to Timbuktu page 94 (author: Rudolph Windsor.

It is becoming very obvious with the preliminary information

that Ghana was indeed a black Jewish kingdom. The first king

of Ghana that accepted Islam was the king of Gao in the year

1010 A.D according to Rudolph Windsors' book; from

Babylon to Timbuktu. This is the truth that is being withheld

from the Hebrews spread out in the Americas and the

Caribbean. Everybody knows that you are Israel, if you tell

them that you are a Hebrew Israelite they will agree with you.

They will never volunteer the information.

MALI EMPIRE: 1200-1500 A.D

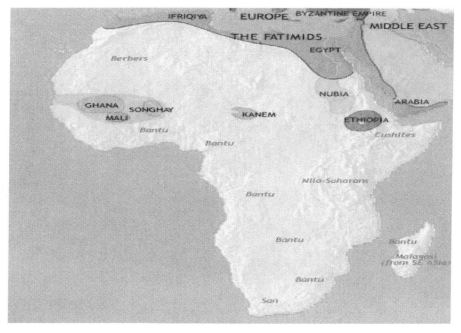

As you can see the empire of Mali grew along side of the empire of Ghana and don't forget they also spoke Bantu. Mali was a Jewish kingdom that was ruled by Mansa Musa the king of Mali. Where is the Windward coast, Wheat coast, Tooth coast, Gold coast or the Slave coast? These places were in the minds of the Kidnapping whites that invaded West Africa, what nation in its right mind would name a piece of its land the Slave Coast? This is the thinking that a Government sponsored education produces, a slave mentality. We will get back to Mansa Musa later, I want to visit some articles that have recently been popping up in the news concerning Hebrew scrolls found at Timbuktu.

MANSA MUSA KING OF MALI

Figure 30 THE RICHEST MAN IN THE WORLD IN THE 14TH CENTURY

CURRENT EVENTS

I have in my possession an article (you can Google this article on the internet) titled, the elusive **libraries of Timbuktu**, this article describes the personal library of one Diadie Haidara. One of the books in Hadauras library is the Tarikh al-Fattash which is a history of the Sudan up to the late sixteenth century. Many of the manuscripts are written in **Hebrew (Bantu)**, that's right Hebrew.

There is another article that should interest you called Islamists in Mali torch library of ancient manuscripts, dated 07/03/2013. The article states that over 3000 ancient manuscripts of Timbuktu have been destroyed and at least one of the ancient manuscripts was written in Hebrew! The solution to this problem is simple, they are finding Hebrew Manuscripts in the ancient abode of the Kingdom of Judah because the people that were sold into the Americas and the Caribbean were Hebrew Israelites who spoke and wrote Hebrew, plain and simple. The evidence on the ground is starting to become overwhelming.

CURRENT EVENTS MAP CONT:

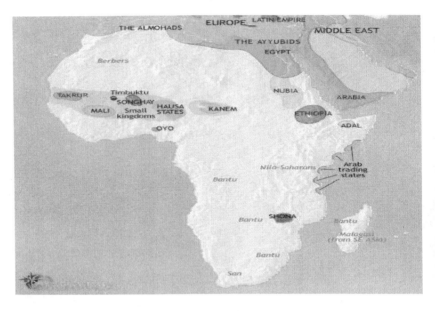

Figure 31 THIS MAP IS DATED TO 1215 A.D

I haven't forgotten about Mansa Musa? Mansa Musa was a devout Muslim and it was said of him that he was the enemy of all Jews. Mansa Musa expelled all Jews from Timbuktu and penalized any Berber who did business with them. **The only way he could expel all Jews is that they would have to have resided there in the first place!**

SONGHAI

1300 A.D-1600 A.D

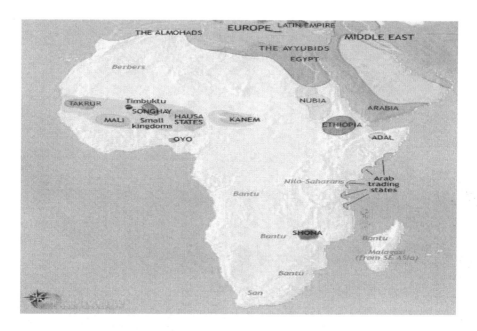

I have to keep this map in front of your face because it has become apparent that the people of Ghana, Mali and Songhai are the same people who gave different names to the small kingdoms located within the empire. There was a king in Songhai whose original name was Mohammed Toure who began to be called by a new name and that was Mohammed Askia. As a result of the rise of the Askia dynasty the Za dynasty of black Hebrew kings was terminated about the year 1492 A.D. The Moroccans (black Moors) invaded Songhai for the wealth and even though the Moors eventually withdrew its army, Songhai would never be the same. After the Moors withdrew from the Sudan the Portuguese, French and English established colonies and took the mineral resources of West Africa. What is the conclusion? For over 1200 years there were black Hebrew Kings ruling over Ghana, Mali and Songhai from one time or another. The West Coast of Africa had an empire that the white historians and their universities never teach nor talk about. This would mean that the children of this North American Slave trade are none other than the children of the Empire! Now that we have placed the children of Israel on the West coast of Africa I would like to deviate from the subject briefly to give you some insight into the origins of the so called White race. **If you want to you can go directly to the stocking of the European colonies** (chapter 11-page 105) **and come back to this chapter later.** The stocking of the European colonies will show you what part of Africa the Portuguese, Spanish, Dutch, French, Germans and English stole or bought their captives from. It will then proceed to show you what part of the America and Caribbean that these helpless peoples were sent to. This next chapter, a brief history of the White race, will show you where the oldest white mummies were found, where white people actually came from, the black Kings of Europe, the black Popes, black Knights and the race war of Europe.

CHAPTER 8 A BRIEF HISTORY OF THE WHITE RACE.

MESOPOTAMIA

Who are these people in the world today who call themselves Europeans or white people? Are they a different race of people? Did they have their origins in the Caucus Mountains? Are they indeed a superior race of people? These are a few of the questions that I will gloss over, meaning you will have to wait on my book that deals with the history of White people. The only history book that gives the origins of the European is the Bible and so I must take you to the 10th chapter of Genesis verses 1-5; verse 1, Now these are the generations of the sons of Noah, Shem, Ham and Japheth. Verse 2 The sons of Japheth: Gomer, Magog, Madai, Javan, Tubal, Meshech and Tiras. Verse 5 by these were the isles of the Gentiles divided in their lands; every one after his tongue after their families, in their Nations. Gomer is the father of the Germans and Magog is the father of the Russians. Madai is the father of the Medes and Javan is the father of the Greeks. Tubal and Meshech is the father of the Moscovites or Russian. The gentiles (White people or Europeans) did not have their origins in the Caucus Mountains of Europe, their father Japheth settled in Shinar or Sumer according to the 11th chapter of Genesis. The 11th chapter of Genesis verses 1-7; Verse 1 And the whole earth was of one language and of one speech. Verse 2 and it came to pass as they journeyed from the East, they found a plain in the land of (Sumer) Shinar and they dwelt there. Look Sumer is in Mesopotamia near the Tigris and Euphrates River, It is in the location of Iraq and Iran. It was from here that the white man sprang and it was from here where we can definitively pick up his footsteps and begin to get a better understanding of this guy.

ASIA

The Bible (11th chapter of Genesis verse 1-9) talks about a time when the Living God came down from the 3rd heaven to disrupt the language of man and to scatter man across the habitable part of the earth. Verse 8 so the Lord scattered them abroad from thence upon the face of all the earth and they left off to build the city. Verse 9 therefore is the name of it called Babel because the Lord did there confound the language of all the earth. It is from Babel that the Lord scattered man abroad upon the face of all the earth. Now there was a time when man only knew of three continents; Asia, Libya (Africa) and Europe but we know that the White race had their orgins in Mesopotamia. So Japheth and his offspring journeyed up into Asia and from there he went into Europe. Two archaeologists (Sven Albert Von Le Coq and Sir Aurel Stein) discovered the remains of Caucasoid mummies carbon dated to around 1800 B.C in the Tarim basin; Xin Jang, China.

THE TARIM MUMMIES

Figure 32 TARIM MUMMIES DISCOVERED AT TARIM BASIN THE OLDEST WHITE MUMMIES EVER FOUND!

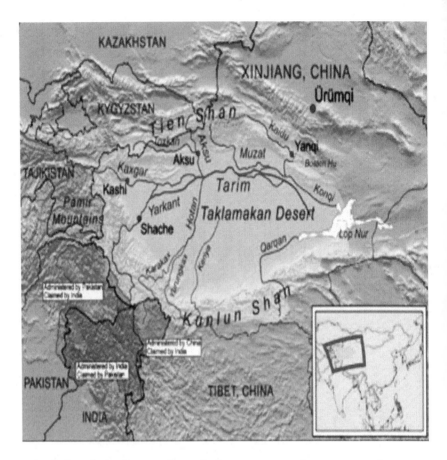

And the date that carbon dating gave to these mummies (1800 B.C) confirms the bibles time frame when man was scattered in the earth at the tower of Babel. You have to remember the further away you get away from Babylon (Epic center) the dates will begin to decline plus travel in those days was like getting a letter from the U.S Postal service. The carbon dating **(1800 B.C)** comes within 443 years **(2243 B.C)**

of the date that the bible gives for the scattering of the sons of Noah in the 11th chapter of Genesis.

BIBLE LONG COUNT		
Creation of Adam 4000 B.C		-400(
Adam was 130 when Seth was born	GENESIS 5:3	130
Seth was 105 when Enos was born	GENESIS 5:6	105
Enos was 90 when Cainan was born	GENESIS 5:9	90
Cainan was 70 when Mahalael born	GENESIS 5:12	70
Mahalael was 65 when Jared was born	GENESIS 5:15	65
Jared was 162 when Enoch was born	GENESIS 5:18	162
Enoch was 65 when Methusalah was born	GENESIS 5:21	65
Methusala was 187 when Lamech was born	GENESIS 5:25	187
Lamech was 182 when Noah was born	GENESIS 5:28	182
Noah 500 when Ham, Shem and Japheth born	GENESIS 5:32	500
NOAH 600 FLOOD ON EARTH		100
THIS THE YEAR OF THE FLOOD -2344 B.C		-234(
Methusalah died the year of the flood! THESE MEN BELOW WERE BORN AFTER THE FLOOD	**NOTABLE!**	-234(
Arpharxad born 2 yrs after flood	GENESIS 11:10	2
Arphaxad WAS 35 when Salah born	GENESIS 11:12	35
Salah was 30 when Eber was born	GENESIS 11:14	30
Eber was 34 when Peleg was born	GENESIS 11:16	34
EARTH DIVIDED PELEG DAYS - 2243 B.C		-224:

The year 2344 B.C is the exact year of the flood and the year that the earth was divided among the sons of Adam was 2243 B.C this is a fact, not fiction.

THE WHITE INVASION OF GREECE

THE GREEK DARK AGES

Akrotiri Frescoe

Figure 33 The black Greeks of Akrotiri, the Procession.

This fresco of black Greeks was taken from an excavation site on Thera, a volcanic island 120 miles Southeast of

Greeces' mainland. This was the site of one of the worlds' greatest eruptions called Akrotiri. See images on next page of black Greeks.

Akrotiri Frescoe

Akrotiri Frescoe

Akrotiri Frescoe

These were the images that emerged from the excavated site at Akrotiri and as you can see these people were black Greeks. This was one of the biggest volcanic eruptions the earth had ever seen, carbon dated to 1500 B.C-1200 B.C. It appears the people are evacuating the city. The reason I showed you these images of the black Greeks was to reinforce the statement that whites invaded a black Greece. The most interesting thing that occurred **when the Whites invaded Greece was that the historians record that all writing stopped and hence Greece experienced a dark age!** This will prove to be the calling card of the white race, I will show you that everywhere and I mean everywhere their feet tread darkness and misery follows. Lets' take a trip to Rome and see what effects if any did these white barbarians have on the Roman empire. I will get back to the subject of this book ,The Negro Question, but in order for us to understand what happened to the West African Captive we must get an understanding of the people who kidnapped us. It is important to try to get a handle on these white Europeans for the sake of understanding why they have taken the attitude toward the colored peoples of the earth. This section is not interested in racial divide, this section has been inserted in this book to validate the claims that I make.

THE WHITE INVASION OF BLACK ROME

THE ROMAN DARK AGES

The European barbarians were the Angles, Saxons, Jutes, Goths, Visisgoths, Vandals, Lombards and Ostrogoths. Your amateur historian knows that in the 5th Century the white barbarians invaded the Roman Empire because of a man by the name of Ghengis Khan. Ghengis Khan was so feared by the barbarians that history records that when Ghengis Khan came across the Volga River that one fourth of Europe migrated southward into the Roman Empire. This migration of barbarians overwhelmed the Romans and eventually the Empire collapsed. One of the questions that the historians never answered was this. Who were the people who lived in these lands before the coming of the white barbarians? Who lived in England (Britain) France, Ireland, Germany and Spain? What does history say that these people looked like? In order for me to answer my own question we must proceed to the archaeological record and the art that it has yielded of that time. I have in my possession images of black Romans and a brown skinned Ghengis Khan, you be the judge.

THE BLACK ROMAN POET VIRGIL

Publius Vergilius Maro (also known as Virgil or Vergil (70 B.C.–19 B.C.)
The great Latin poet Virgil, holding a volume on which is written the Aeneid. On either side stand the two muses: "Clio" (history) and "Melpomene" (tragedy). The mosaic, which dates from the 3rd Century A.D, was discovered in the Hadrumetum in Sousse, Tunisia and is now on display in the Bardo Museum in Tunis, Tunisia.

This is an authentic image of Virgil the famous Roman poet and the fresco was dated back to 200 A.D. If I was you I would take this book to school and ask your professors about these images. Ask them why haven't you never been exposed

to them and see what he says.

ROMAN CITIZENS

Baccanti Tomb, Tarquinia

This image is of the ancient Etruscans' and these are the images

that was left behind of the ancient Romans. These were some of the

people that lived in the Roman Empire before the coming of Ghengis

Khan. The Roman Empire was an Empire built up on the same

experiment as the Americas, there was no such thing as race. Racism

74

is an 20th century invention, as you will see from the so called Renaisance period. White barbarians, out of fear, begin to migrate South toward the Holy Roman Empire.

GHENGIS KHAN

Genghis Khan

Figure 34 GHENGIS KHAN
SCROLL FOUND NATIONAL PALACE MUSEUM TAPEI

This is the man who made Europe get up off its axis and flood the Roman Empire. As you can see Genghis Khan is a brown skinned man, not a white man as the History Channel and Hollywood portrays him. In fact on the next page is an image of his grandson Kublai Khan and he is also a brown skinned man. This is

75

the reason that it is important that we push for a rewriting of ancient world history. In fact this book is the rewriting of world history according to the facts.

Figure 35BROWN SKINNED KUBLAI KHAN THE GRANDSON OF GHENGIS KHAN

**Figure 36 GERMAN TAPESTRY WILD MEN AND MOORS
1400 A.D**

This is a snapshot of what the black Europeans experienced

during the 100 year war (1334-1453) in Europe when these

white Barbarians overran black Europe. You think that this

image is deep? Keep reading and you will really freak out!

CHAPTER 9: THE BLACK KINGS AND POPES OF EUROPE

BLACK RUSSIAN KING MIRIAN 3RD

Mirian III was a king of Kartli (modern Georgia). A contemporary to the Roman emperor Constantine I (306–337). Kartli was the successor state of the ancient kingdom of Colchis: (made famous by Herodotus' description of it's people - they are black-skinned and have woolly hair), and the ancient kingdom of Eastern Iberia.

17th century mural from the Svetitskhoveli cathedral in Georgia.

According to the early medieval Georgian annals and hagiography, Mirian was the first Christian king of Iberia, converted through the ministry of Nino, a Cappadocian female missionary. He is credited with establishment of Christianity as his kingdom's state religion and is regarded by the Georgian Orthodox Church as a saint.

BLACK HUNGARIAN KING BELA

King Bela on the flight from the Mongols.
The Mongols in Hungary 1241. Széchényi National Library, Budapest, fol. 63 recto, Inv. no. Clmae 404
(the picture is of a 19th century reproduction). From the Chronicum Pictum in Hungary's National Libra

Painting of Emperor Alexius I,
from a Greek manuscript in the Vatican library

WHEN THE PAPACY MOVED FROM ROME TO AVIGNON

It has been recorded in the history of the Europeans that the Papacy did indeed move from the Papish estates in Rome to France from the years of 1305-1378. This has also been phrased as the Babylonian captivity of the Papacy, which is an allusion to the 70 year captivity of Judah in Babylon.

Saint Catherine of Siena before the Pope at Avignon (Pope Gregory XI), by Giovanni di Paolo (1460)

This is the image (snap shot) that comes to us from antiquity of the blackness of the Avignon Popes that moved their residency from the Papal estates in Rome to come under the protection of the black French (Frankish) King Charles the fifth! These black Popes had to move to France because of the tide of racial hate that had begun to spread across the continent of Europe. On hindsight their departure from Rome signaled the beginning of the coming **ONE HUNDERED YEAR RACE WARS IN EUROPE!** In English the genocide of the black European.

BLACK HOLY ROMAN EMPEROR KING

LEOPOLD1

Holy Roman Emperor Leopold I - House of Habsburg

81

Holy Roman Emperor Leopold I, 1640-1705

Figure 37 COIN DEPICTING LEOPOLD

This is an image of King Leopold the 1st who just so happens to be a black Holy Roman German emperor. I know these images can be a little disconcerting but these images had their origination in Europe. In fact the Habsburg house is the house that the next Holy Roman Emperor will come out of. The most interesting point that I would like to make is that the Habsburgs of Europe are now white! How that happened will be saved for another book.

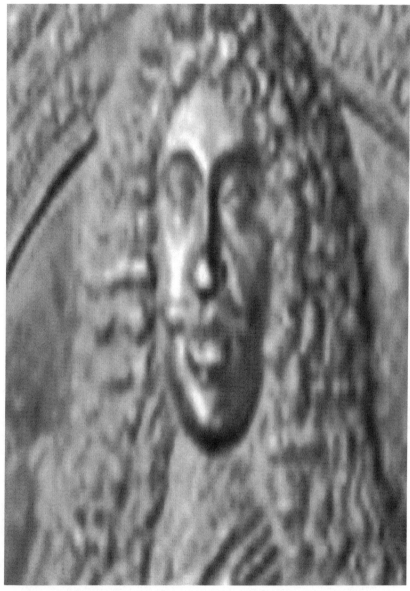

Figure 38 Holy Roman Emperor King Leopold 1 1640-1705

This image was taken off of a coin that was minted by King Leopold of himself and he had himself depicted as a black man with nappy locks. See the next page of an image of his mother Maria of Austria.

83

Figure 39 Maria Habsburg of Austria 1528-1603

This is Queen Maria Habsburg of Austria who just so happens to be the mother of King Leopold 1 on pages 81 & 82 and so far the entire family is black. I want you to go to the next page to see an image of Maria Habsburgs' father and King Leopold 1st grandfather, Charles the 5th.

A panel from the painting in the Larco museum in Lima Peru, depicting the Inca Emperors. This panel shows the last sev and the subsequent first European Emperor of the Inca: Holy Roman Emperor Charles V (Carlos Quinto) as the 15th Inca

The painting can be dated circa 1800: because the last two entries are Carlos Tercero (Charles III) as the 24th Inca Emp Carlos Quarto (Charles IV) House of Bourbon, as the 25th Inca Emperor. Charles IV reigned as king of Spain from Decen March 19, 1808 (abdicated in favor of his son Fernand VII).

This is an image of Charles the 5th that has been recorded and kept in the Larco museum in Lima Peru. From left to right, the last image on the right is the true picture of Charles the 5th the Holy Roman German Emperor, the father of Maria of Austria.. He is depicted as a black man. I have enlarged his image on the next page so that you can see the blackness of this King. I want to make this plain to you the reader, history is repeat with White men and women who risked life and limb to help the so called Negro; Abraham Lincoln, John Brown, John Kennedy, Bobby Kennedy and those whites who helped with the underground railroad to name a few. We are grateful to you Europeans who believe in righteousness and the truth.

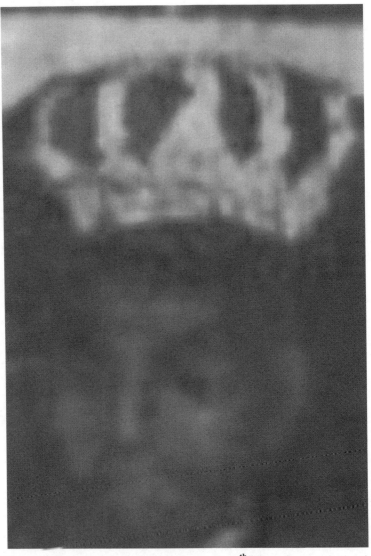

Figure 40 This is an image of Charles the 5th taken from painting in Lima Peru Museum being depicted as a black King.

This is the grandfather of King Leopold the 1st and the father of Queen Maria Habsburg of Austria. The entire family is black, need I further proof?

KING CHARLEMAGNE BLACK HOLY ROMAN EMPEROR

Charlemagne - Karlštejn Castle, Czech Republic.
Charlemagne: Carolus Magnus, meaning Charles the Great.
(742–814) was King of the Franks from 768 and Emperor of
the Romans from 800 to his death in 814.

This portrait of Charlemagne comes to you from Karlstejn Castle in
the Czech Republic, it appears that the brothers in Eastern Europe
had no problem with the truth concerning the black Emperors. The
symbol on his shield is the symbol (Two black eagles) of the black
Holy Roman German Empire of Europe. This is a fact not fiction, the
only fiction is in our modern day history books, the real history of
Europe is a black history! After the Renaisance period in Europe
everything that was black became white, including the symbol of the
Habsburg empire. The Eagle is now painted white instead of black.

Charlemagne Shrine - Commissioned by Henry IV, (1054). Palatine Chapel, UNESCO Site

It appears that the French Kings according to antiquity (ancient history) were black even from the beginning of their reign. This is an image of Charlemagne and if this guy isn't black then the sun dosen't rise in the east and set in the west.

BLACK ROMAN EMPEROR FREDERICK 1 BARBOSSA

Holy Roman Emperor Frederick I Barbarossa (1122-1190), receives credentials from ambassadors of Venice, miniature, early fifteenth century, Museo Correr Venice.

So far as late as the 12th century the Kings of Europe are being depicted as black by the Europeans themselves, these are not forgeries. Could these be the Jews that were carted off into the captivity by Vespasian Caesar?

I want to make this very clear that these pictures are authentic images of these black European Kings. Most of these images are being warehoused at the Vatican Library. You can validate these images from the reference section of this book.

THE BLACK POPES OF BRITAIN, IRELAND & EUROPE!

Saint Catherine of Siena before the Pope at Avignon (Pope Gregory XI), by Giovanni di Paolo (1460)

I am of the same opinion that you are…..I don't know what to make of the fact that the Kings and Popes were black…..it is bleeping unbelievable but the images don't lie. We have traveled to the 15th century and the Europeans are depicting their Kings and Popes as black men!

ICONS OF ALL SAINTS OF BRITISH ISLES AND IRELAND!

Figure 41 This image was found at Saint Seraphim Church in Walsingham, Norfolk England

I bet your eyes are jumping out of your head now! Not only do they depict their Kings, Princes, and Nuns black they also present Jesus as being black. I know the images are small but it is one of the pieces of the puzzle! See blown up image on next page.

This image was isolated from the image of page 86 and enlarged to show you the black Kings and Princes of Britain and Ireland. The images don't lie, there was a time when the Royalty of Europe was none other than the black man. If you are a Hebrew Israelite and you know brother Bouie, you can see that a couple of these guys look like him.

Painted panel from the outer right-hand wing of a polyptych. The young man wears the crown of a nobleman and carries the red and white military pennant and shield of the Holy Roman Empire, circa 1447. From Wiener Neustadt Abbey, Stefansdom, Vienna. (In typical Albino fashion, he is claimed to be Saint Maurice).

The revelation that you should be getting is simple, the Kings, Popes and knights were black people but why would the white European try to hide the truth about the Negro rulership in Europe?

The old timers have a saying…there is a rat on the line and I am in agreement.

Saint Reinoldus (also Reynald of Cologne): since the 11th Century, has been the patron saint of the city of Dortmund, via transfer from Cologne to Dortmund, allegedly by Saint Anno II (1010-1075) who was Archbishop of Cologne. Reinoldus was one of four sons of the Earl of Haemon and his wife Aya, and was the nephew of Charlemagne. A military conflict with Charlemagne caused Reinold and his brothers to flee, they became known as the four Haimonskinder. Reinold built the impregnable fortress of Montalban, which was besieged for years by Charles, but he could not conquer it. A plea was made to Charles I by his sister Ayas to spare her sons, which Charles granted, but at a high price.

Text accompanying this statue at Magdeburg Cathedral: "this is the oldest known image depicting Saint Maurice as a Moor, the statue was carved around 1250 and shows him as an armored knight."

CHAPTER 10   THE EUROPEAN BLACK PLAGUE

FACT OR FICTION

What is the real truth about the disappearance of all of these black Europeans? Did they die from the result of the so called black plague or was the black population of the Holy Roman German empire the black plague? These are some statistics from the European wars;

France 100 year war, 1337-1453; at the end of the 100 year war 50% of Frances' black population was dead!

Germany 30 year war, 1618-1648-;Black Holy Roman German Empire verses England, France (now controlled by white Europeans) Russia, Dutch, Sweden, Transylnavnia and Hesse Palatinate. When the war ended 40% of the black German population was killed.

Britain civil war 1642-1651; black Britains fought against the white Britains andn 4% of the British population died, the Scottish population decreased by 6% and the black irish population decreased by 41%.

It appears that the so called black plague in Europe was nothing but a race war in which the White Europeans finally evicted the black ruling class from the European continent. The images don't lie, these black Kings, Popes, and Knights existed and they were wise to keep portraits of themselves else we would have never known. To solidify my argument I have in my possession a letter written by none other than Benjamin Franklin himself concerning the existence of the black German European.

> **Title : America as a land of opportunity**
> **Author: Benjamin Franklin**
> **Year:1751**
> **Subject: Why increase the sons of Africa in America**
> **Title: America as a land of opportunity**

And since Detachments of English from Britain sent to America, will have their Places at Home so soon supply'd and increase so largely here;

why should the Palatine Boors [Germans] be suffered to swarm into our Settlements, and by herding together establish their Language and Manners to the Exclusion of ours? Why should Pennsylvania, founded by the English, become a Colony of Aliens, who will shortly be so numerous **as to Germanize us** instead of our Anglifying them, and will never adopt our Language or Customs, **any more than they can acquire our Complexion**. **Hey Benjamin, Franklin can you translate what you said into modern English? In English Benjamin is telling you that the Germans were a black race of people!**

SWARTHY EUROPEAN SLANG=BLACK

TAWNEY EUROPEAN SLANG= BLACK

Which leads me to add one Remark: That the Number of purely white People in the World is proportionably very small. All Africa is **black or tawny.** Asia chiefly tawny. America (exclusive of the new Comers) wholly so. **And in Europe, the Spaniards, French Italians, Russians and Swedes, are generally of what we call a swarthy Complexion; as are the Germans also,** the **Saxons only excepted, who with the English, make the principal Body of White People on the Face of the Earth.** I could wish their Numbers were increased. And while we are, as I may call it, Scouring our Planet, by clearing America of Woods, and so making this Side of our Globe reflect a brighter Light to the Eyes of Inhabitants in mars or Venus, why should we in the Sight of Superior Beings, darken its People? why increase the Sons of Africa, by Planting them in America **(Benjamin Franklin is not talking about the West African captive, he is talking about the black European coming to America)** where we have so fair an Opportunity, **by excluding all Blacks and Tawneys,** of increasing the lovely White and Red? But perhaps I am partial to the complexion of my Country, for such Kind of Partiality is natural to Mankind.

Benjamin Franklin is asking why should the blacks of the Holy Roman German empire be admitted into the 13 colonies and goes on to admit what nations in Europe were black, check out the list; Spain, Italians, French, Russians and the Swedes. He says that white people on earth was only a small number and that the British and the Saxons was that number! What are we to conclude from this section on the white race? This is a diabolical plot by the White powers that be to hide the fact that Black Kings ruled Europe for at least.....1500 years, from 300 A.D to 1800 A.D!

FURTHER EVIDENCE

Now lets examine the mystery in a rational manner, why would the Europeans **blot out** (OMITT) from his history books the existence of black Kings, black Popes, black Knights and the fact that black Europeans were shipped into the slave trade to America? Could it be (conjecture) that these black Kings and Black Popes was none other than Judah , Benjamin and Levi who Titus Caesar had taken captive across the Meditterean in 70 A.D? Could it be that the seed of Judah had taken the dominion in Europe just like the seed did in the Americas' and the Caribbean? One thing is for certain the blacks of the Holy Roman German Empire were deported to the North American colonies **per the letter that Benjamin Franklin wrote** and per this peculiar letter written beneath.

LETTER: SLAVE SHIPS FROM EUROPE :

Not to forget the Blacks from continental Europe: So far we have **identified three Ships** which regularly transported Blacks from Germany and Holland where they were gathered for the transatlantic trip.

The Jamaica

The Glasgow

The Marlborough.

TYPICAL ENTRY:

Ship Jamaica Galley Rotterdam to Cowes in England to Philadelphia 7 February 1738
Ship Glasgow Walter Sterling Commander from Rotterdam but last from Cows in England. Qualified the 9th Day of September 1738
Ship Marlborough, Thomas Bell, Master. Qualified Sept. 23, 1741. From Rotterdam, but last from Cowes.

Carried a cargos of **Palatine Males** (Electoral Palatinate or County **Palatine of the Rhine**, a historic state of the Black Holy Roman Empire).

They were required to take this oath

* Oath of Allegiance: We Subscribers Natives and late Inhabitants of **the** Palatinate **(Black Holy Roman GermanEmpire)** upon the **Rhine and places adjacent,** having transported
our Selves and Families into **the Province of Pennsylvania**, a Colony Subject to the Crown of Great Britain, in hopes and **expectation of finding a retreat and peaceable Settlement** therein DO solemnly promise and engage that we will be faithfull and bear true Allegiance to **his present Majesty King George the Second** and his Successon Kings of Great Britain and will be faithfull to the Proprietor of this Province and that we will demean our Selves peaceably to all his Majesties Subjects, and Strictly observe and conform to the Laws of England and of this Province to the utmost of our power and best of our understanding.

Note:

White Europeans will claim that these were Whites, but does "demean ourselves peaceably to all his Majesties Subjects" sound like an oath Protestant allies or Whites would have to take?

A mediaeval miniature of Edward III of England. The king is wearing a blue garter, of the Order of the Garter, over his plate armour.
ca. between 1430 and 1440 - before 1450

This image is of King Edward 3rd of England and he is not a white man as was taught in your history books. This image is almost two hundred older than the letter that George Washington wrote back to England concerning the arriving black Europeans to the Americas. WOW!

King George III

You all know the story of the American revolution and the reason I know you do, is because you have been taught more about the white man and his history than you have of your own. This is a true image of King George the 3rd and he doesn't look like a white man, in fact he looks very much like a red bone. For those of you who don't know what a red bone is, it is an adjective; a word that describes something and in this case redbone describes the color of King George the 3rd. On the next page is a image of his wife **(Wifey)** the most beautiful Queen Charlotte of Germany and this woman is a red bone with nappy hair! See for yourself.

Charlotte of Mecklenburg-Strelitz of Germany (19 May 1744-17 Nov. 1818). Sophia Charlotte was born on 19 May 1744. She was the youngest daughter of Duke Charles Louis Frederick of Mecklenburg-Strelitz, Prince of Mirow and his wife Princess Elizabeth Albertine of Saxe-Hildburghausen. Mecklenburg-Strelitz was a small north German duchy in the Holy Roman Empire. She was a granddaughter of Adolf Frederick II, Duke of Mecklenburg-Strelitz, by his third wife, Christiane Emilie Antonie, Princess of Schwarzburg-Sondershausen. Her father's elder half brother reigned from 1708 to 1753 as Adolf Friedrich III.

In Britain she was the Queen consort of the United Kingdom as the wife of King George III. She was also the electress consort of Hanover in the Holy Roman Empire (Germany) until the promotion of her husband to King of Hanover on 12 October 1814, which made her Queen consort of Hanover. George III and Charlotte had 15 children, 13 of whom survived to adulthood.

THE AVAILABLE DATA

It is clear that from the available data that we had two converging groups of black captives descending on the Americas and the Caribbean, the one group came from West Africa and the other group came from Europe. There can be only one conclusion from the data that is available and that is....there is a major cover up on both sides of the Atlantic but the question that keeps nagging at me is why? Why are the Europeans afraid to teach the truth about our black history on both sides of the Atlantic Ocean and the Mediterranean sea? What are these people afraid of? I know that was a lot of information but I thought that it was necessary to get an idea concerning these people who call themselves Europeans. This was the state of mind of the white European that converged on Libya (Africa), they had just exterminated the blacks off of the continent of Europe and it appears that they set about to do the same thing in Africa but they had one huge problem.....the brothers on the continent was willing to fight to the death, on the continent of West Africa and all over the Americas and the Caribbean, wherever they were dropped off! And from this backdrop and from this vantage point we proceed to the section titled the stocking the Americas and the Caribbean by the European colonizers. We are at that point when Judah and Levi have been stolen from West Africa and colonized all over the Americas and the Caribbean.

THE STOCKING OF THE EUROPEANCOLONIES

This section of this book will deal specifically with what geographical location on West Africa the Europeans colonized and where they placed the Africans that they either captured or purchased. You will have to remember that the captives in each of the European colonies came from their colonized West African colonies. This is critical in keeping track of where the captives came from in the Americas and the Caribbean. I have provided you with a ledger to help you understand the spreadsheet that I have prepared for you.

FROM AFRICA: means the Spanish, English, Portuguese, French, Dutch took their captives from these parts of Africa. Each European colonizing power took captives from a region in West Africa and stocked his colonies in the Americas and Caribbean with his captives.

TO: means that the Spanish, English, Portuguese, French, Dutch took their captives to; Their South America, Central America, North America and Caribbean colonies.

This ledger will also tell you what nations in the Americas and Caribbean that the Europeans colonized their captives to.

CHAPTER 11 THE STOCKING OF THE SPANISH

COLONIES:

THE SPANISH TOOK THEIR CAPTIVES FROM KINGDOM OF JUDAH.

	SPANISH COLONIES	
FROM	**AFRICA**	
	WHYDAH/JUDAH	
JUDAH/LEV	CAPER VERDE ISLAN	
LEVI	GOLD COAST/ASHANTI	
	ANGOLA/CONGO	
	GAMBIA	
	NEW GUINEA	
	NIGERIA	
	SPANISH COLONIES	
TO	**SOUTH AMERICA**	
JUDAH	GUYANA	
LEVI	VENEZUELA	
	COLUMBIA	
	ECUADOR	
	PERU	
	CHILE	
	ARGENTINA	
	URUGUAY	
	BOLIVIA	
	SPANISH COLONIES	
TO	**CENTRAL AMERICA**	
JUDAH	**MEXICO**	
LEVI	**BELIZE**	
	GUATEMALA	
	EL SALVADOR	
	COSTA RICA	

HONDURAS
NICARAQUA
PANAMA

SPAIN CONTINUED:

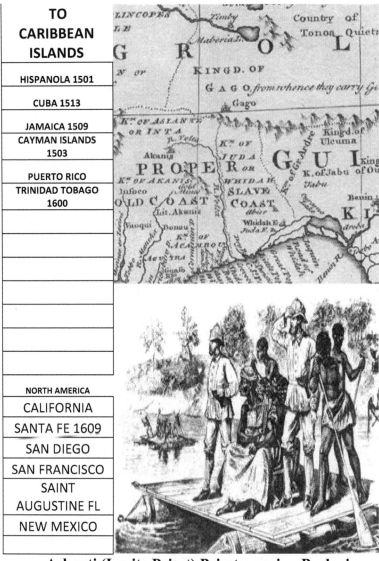

TO CARIBBEAN ISLANDS
HISPANOLA 1501
CUBA 1513
JAMAICA 1509
CAYMAN ISLANDS 1503
PUERTO RICO
TRINIDAD TOBAGO 1600

NORTH AMERICA
CALIFORNIA
SANTA FE 1609
SAN DIEGO
SAN FRANCISCO
SAINT AUGUSTINE FL
NEW MEXICO

Ashanti (Levite Priest) Priest crossing Prah river

with British war correspondant.

The Spanish imported captives from the Kingdom of Judah

on the West coast of Africa to their colonies in South America:

TO VENEZUELA

**Figure 42 JOSE LEONARDO CHIRINO
LED A SLAVE REVOLT IN VENEZUELA AND WAS
HANGED.**

Figure 43 IMAGE OF BENKOS BIOHO
THE KING OF MANTUNA

He was the first African rebel to engage in guerrilla warfare and he declared Mantuna independent.

**Figure 44ALONSO DE ILLESCAS REBEL HERO OF
ECUADOR 1553 A.D**

Figure 45 3 CHIEFS (3DONS) OF ESMERALDAS BLACKS
IMAGE FOUND IN LARCO MUSEUM; LIMA, PERU

TO PERU

Figure 46 MARIA ELENA MOYANO
Peruvian activist murdered by Maoist shining path party. This
caused a public outcry in Peru.

TO CHILE

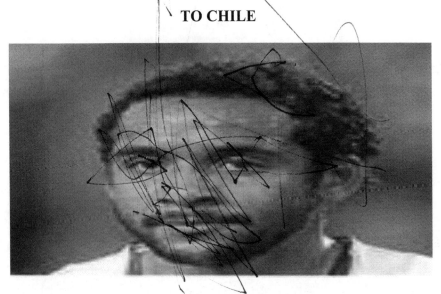

Figure 47 JEAN BEAUSEJOUR.
Is attempting to bring international attention to a shameful fact,
that in his country the African Chileans are not recognized on the
national census.

TO ARGENTINIA

Figure 48 FIDEL NADAL
International Reggae singer from Argentina
In Argentina blacks of African descent are not recognized as
existing in the country.

TO URUGUAY

Figure 49 NOELIA MACIEL
Noelia Maciel is a human rights leader in Uruguay who is
attempting to bring attention to the human rights violations in her
country of black Uruguayans.

AND FINALLY TO BOLIVIA

Figure 50 KING BONAFICIO PINEDO

A descendant of King Bonifaz of Senegal was crowned King of
Bolivia. When he died his son Julio Pinedo became King.

Figure 51Afrom Bolivian King Julio Pinedo

The crowning at the countries capital was to make the
world aware of the African Bolivian presence in Bolivia.

It appears that there is a conspiracy among the South American whites to erase the existence of the former black captives. To the Hebrew brothers and sisters in South America your true identity has been known for years among the European elite. The kings of Europe (King Edward of England and King Louis 15th of France) knew who you were when they sent Emanuel Bowen in 1747 to map out your land in Guinea West Africa. Their newspapers, Universities, Museums and the Catholic Church know full well that you are the children of Israel spoken of in the Bible. It appears that the prophecy concerning you has come full circle **(Psalm 83:1-4), that they have tried to cut off the name of Israel; that the name Israel would be no more in remembrance**. This is what is going on with the Chilean government and the Argentinean government refusal to recognize (Census) the African populations among them. It was written of you in the book of Deuteronomy (Deuteronomy 28:68) that the Lord would bring you into Egypt again with ships by the way whereof I spoke unto thee. Thou shall see it no more again: There you shall be sold unto your enemies for bondmen and bondwomen and no man shall buy you. No other people in this hemisphere can make that boast, you and we in America are the only people brought to the Americas as captives. We have been sold as bond men and bond women and we have never returned to the land of Africa. The God of Israel has not forgotten you it has been said of God concerning you in the book of Isaiah (Isaiah 49:14,15 and16); That Zion said," the Lord has forgotten me. Verse 15 Can a woman forget her suckling child that she should not have compassion on the son of her womb? Yes they may forget yet will in not forget you. Verse 16 Behold I have engraven thee in the palms of my hands. Your walls are continually before me!

SPANISH CENTRAL AMERICA

TO MEXICO

Figure 52GASPAR YANGA, THE PRINCE OF GABON

A Prince from the Royal house of Gabon, West Africa, Gaspar
was captured in war and taken to Mexico as a slave, he led a
successful slave revolt in Mexico and founded the free town of
Yanga, it appears that Yanga named the town after the River in West
Africa, Gabon.

Figure 53 IN MEMORY OF WILL AND SHARPER.

Will and Sharper led a slave revolt in Belize but as usual there is very little information concerning this galliant act.

The first African captives arrived in Guatemala in 1524 and of that there is little information. We do know that these Hebrew brothers fought in 1611 and helped defeat the Maroons of Tutale.

TO EL SALVADOR

**Figure 54 THE STATUE OF JOSE SIMEON CANAS
THE ENSCRIPTION CALLS HIM A LIBERATOR. CITY OF
ZACATEOCOLUCA EL SALVADOR.**

What I am starting to find is that there isn't much history on
the brothers and sisters that were held captive in South and Central
America....interesting.

Figure 55 COSTA RICAN BLACK WOMEN

Costa Rica boasts a population of only 130,000 persons of African descent omitting the children born of mixed descent. This appears to be a reoccurring trend in the Americas and the Caribbean and that trend is to wipe out the memory of these black Hebrew Israelites.

Figure 56 KENIA MARTINEZ MISS UNIVERSE HONDURAS

The Hondurian government national census records 200,000 people of African descent thereby ignoring the children of mixed descent. The trend to erase the existence of the black Hebrew Israelites that were dropped off by the European colonizers continues.

Figure 57 NICARAUGA HAS THE HIGHEST AFRICAN POPULATION OF AFRICAN DESCENT IN CENTRAL AMERICA

TO PANAMA

Figure 58 IN MEMORY OF KING BAYANO

I couldn't find any images of Bayano but it was reported that Bayano was a Mandinka Prince from West Africa. Bayano was captured in war and sold into the Panamanian captivity. He led a successful revolt against the Spanish in Panama. He along with forty two of his men went with a delegation to seek peace with the Spanish. The Spanish gave a great big dinner and poisoned Bayano with forty two of his men. Bayano was captured and sent to Peru and then to Spain where he died.

To the Hebrew brothers and sisters in Central America your true identity has been known for years among the European elite. The kings of Europe (King Edward of England and King Louis 15th of France) knew who you were when they sent Emanuel Bowen in 1747 to map out your land in Guinea West Africa. Their newspapers, Universities, Museums and the Catholic Church know full well that you are the children of Israel spoken of in the Bible. It appears that the prophecy concerning you has come full circle **(Psalm 83:1-4), that they have tried to cut off the name of Israel; that the name Israel would be no more in remembrance.** This is what is going on with the governments of Chile, Argentina, Honduras and Costa Rica refusal to recognize (Census) the African populations among them. It was written of you in the book of Deuteronomy (Deuteronomy 28:68) that the Lord would bring you into Egypt again with ships by the way whereof I spoke unto thee. Thou shall see it no more again: There you shall be sold unto your enemies for bondmen and bondwomen an no man shall buy you. No other people in this hemisphere can make that boast, you and us in America are the only people brought to the

Americas as captives. We have been sold as bond men and bond women and we have never returned to the land of Africa. The God of Israel has not forgotten you it has been said of God concerning you in the book of Isaiah (Isaiah 49:14,15 and16); That Zion said," the Lord has forgotten me. Verse 15 Can a woman forget her suckling child that she should not have compassion on the son of her womb? Yes they may forget yet will in not forget you. Verse 16 Behold I have engraven thee in the palms of my hands. Your walls are continually before me! The most high has not forgotten you and this is the hour of your visitation! Rejoice o thee that was barren for your creator is in the midst of thee! For a small moment (Isaiah 54:7,8) have I forsaken thee; But with great mercies will I gather thee. Verse 8 in a little wrath I hid my face from thee for a moment; But with everlasting kindness will I have mercy on thee, says the Lord! Part of our problem in the Americas is that we have allowed ourselves and our off spring to be taught by the very people who hate us the most. How on earth can you wake up out of this deep sleep when your enemy is giving you a concoction called amnesia? He is deliberately teaching you lies about yourself and the history of the world so that he can maintain dominance over you.

TO THE HEBREWS IN THE SPANISH CARIBBEAN

To the seed of the brothers and sisters who were transported from the kingdoms of Judah (Senegal, Guinea, Gold Coast, Slave Coast, Angola, Congo, Gambia, Ashanti and Nigeria in West Africa to;

TO DOMINICAN REPUBLIC/ HISPANOLA

Figure 59 ULISES HEUREUX

Black general of Hispanola/Dominican Republic, who became President in 1882, his Presidency lasted until the year of his assassination in 1889.

Figure 60 THE MAMBI ARMY

These African Cubans defeated the Spanish in two wars of
independence, 1868-1878 and 1895-1898. Mamba is a Congo word.

TO PUERTO RICO

Figure 61 IN MEMORY OF MARCOS XIORRO

He led an unsuccessful slave revolt in 1821. He was helped by Mario and Narciso who ere executed but the fate of Marcos Xiorro is not known. Is this the Xiorro of the Hollywood movies Zorro?

TO JAMAICA

Figure 62SAM SHARPE, THE PREACHER

A Jamaican preacher who led a slave uprising against the British in 1831, he was captured and publically executed.

126

Figure 63 KING (CHIEF) TACKY

In remembrance of Tacky who was a chief of Ghana. Tacky was captured off of the West coast of Africa and sold into Jamaica. Tacky led a revolt in Jamaica killing 60 whites before being captured and eventually executed

TO CAYMAN ISLANDS

Although we have evidence that in an 1802 census there were 933 residents on the Cayman Islands. Of the 933 residents 545 were African captives from the west coast of Africa. In 1834 another census was taken in which there were 950 African captives counted. The African history on this island is vague but base on what you have read so far you shouldn't be surprised.

TO TOBAGO

Figure 64 IN MEMORY OF: SANDY LONG

Brother Sandy Long along with 6 other black Africans led a revolt in Tobago that lasted 6 weeks. In the aftermath Sandy with his cohorts were executed.

TRINIDAD

This was the only slave insurrection that is recorded in Trinidads' history and it occurred in 1822. The escaped captives killed all of the whites in the surrounding countryside and then marched on the Port of Spain, killing and pillaging along the way. Three of the rebels that were caught were beheaded and their heads were displayed in the town square.

A LETTER TO THE HEBREWS IN THE SPANISH CARIBBEAN

The God of Israel has not forgotten you it has been said of God concerning you in the book of Isaiah (Isaiah 49:14,15and16); That Zion said," the Lord has forgotten me.

Verse 15 Can a woman forget her suckling child that she should not have compassion on the son of her womb? Yes they may forget yet will in not forget you. Verse 16 Behold I have en graven thee in the palms of my hands. Your walls are continually before me! The most high has not forgotten you and this is the hour of your visitation! Rejoice o thee that was barren for your creator is in the midst of thee! For a small moment (Isaiah 54:7,8) have I forsaken thee; But with great mercies will I gather thee Verse 8 in a little wrath I hid my face from thee for a moment; But with everlasting kindness will I have mercy on thee, says the Lord! That is correct the message to the brotherhood is the same. Whoever touches you touches the apple of my eye says the Lord.

CHAPTER 12   THE STOCKING OF THE

FRENCH COLONIES:

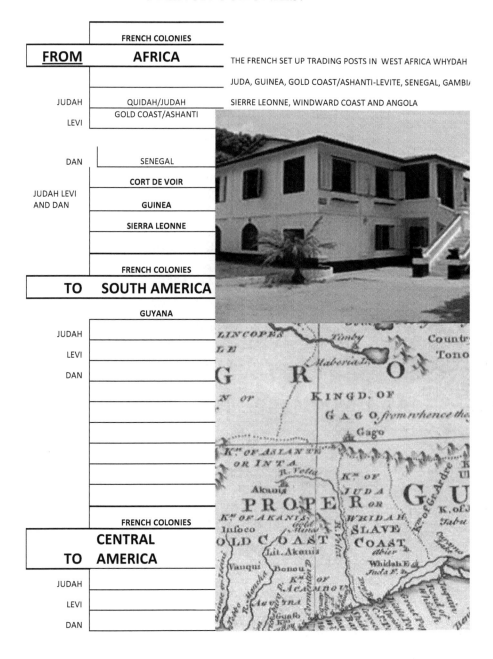

	FRENCH COLONIES	
FROM	**AFRICA**	THE FRENCH SET UP TRADING POSTS IN WEST AFRICA WHYDAH
		JUDA, GUINEA, GOLD COAST/ASHANTI-LEVITE, SENEGAL, GAMBIA
JUDAH	QUIDAH/JUDAH	SIERRE LEONNE, WINDWARD COAST AND ANGOLA
LEVI	GOLD COAST/ASHANTI	
DAN	SENEGAL	
	CORT DE VOIR	
JUDAH LEVI AND DAN	GUINEA	
	SIERRA LEONNE	
	FRENCH COLONIES	
TO	**SOUTH AMERICA**	
	GUYANA	
JUDAH		
LEVI		
DAN		
	FRENCH COLONIES	
	CENTRAL	
TO	**AMERICA**	
JUDAH		
LEVI		
DAN		

HAITI

CARIBBEAN ISLANDS		
HAITI		
GUADALUPE		
TO		
NORTH AMERICA		
SOUTH CAROLINA		
DETROIT		
FLORIDA/ FORT CAROLINA		
TEXAS/ FORT ST LOUIS		
ARKANSAS		
MOBILE ALABAMA		
ST LOUIS MISSOURI		
ILLINOIS/ PEORIA ILL		
LOUISIANA		
MISSISSIPI		

Figure 65 L TOUSSANT OVERTURE

THE PRINCE FROM ARADA, BENIN

Because I relied on the teachings of the Europeans in grade school, high school and college I never took the time out to see where Toussants' family came from. To my amazement his father (Gaou Ginu) was a chief/King from Benin, West Africa. This would mean that the young man Toussaint was a prince who became King of Haiti!

GUADALUPE

Figure 66 GENERAL LOUIS DELGRES

General Delgres Led a resistance movement against Napoleons' reoccupation of Guadalupe. The French had ended slavery in Guadalupe but when Napoleon came into power he reinstituted the institution. General Louis with 400 men and women ignited gun stores killing themselves and some French soldiers rather than to be taken alive as slaves.

A LETTER TO THE HEBREWS IN FRENCH CARIBBEAN

The God of Israel has not forgotten you it has been said of God concerning you in the book of Isaiah (Isaiah 49:14,15and16); That Zion said," the Lord has forgotten me. Verse 15 Can a woman forget her suckling child that she should not have compassion on the son of her womb? Yes they may forget yet will in not forget you. Verse 16 Behold I have en graven thee in the palms of my hands. Your walls are continually before me! The most high has not forgotten you and this is the hour of your visitation! Rejoice o thee that was barren for your creator is in the midst of thee! For a small moment (Isaiah 54:7,8) have I forsaken thee; But with great mercies will I gather thee Verse 8 in a little wrath I hid my face from thee for a moment; But with everlasting kindness will I have mercy on thee, says the Lord! That is correct the message to the brotherhood is the same.

TO THE HEBREWS IN THE FRENCH

NORTH AMERICA

To the brothers and sisters in British North America

(Black Hebrew Israelites) I would like to refresh your

memory concerning ships that landed at the mouth of the

Mississippi River.

> There is a publication written at Louisiana state University
> Titled: Creole New Orleans
> Race and Americanization
> Edited by R. Hirsch and Joseph Logsdon
> Louisiana State University Press
> Baton Rouge and London

On page 67 of this publication are the notes of a white

slaver recalling the inventory of human beings on a cargo

ship…..lets' see what he writes. He writes that " sixteen slave

trading ships arrived from the Senegal region. <u>**Six ships came**</u>

<u>**from Juda**</u> and landed at the mouth of the Mississipi and in

<u>1731 one ship form **Juda** landed 464 slaves</u> at the mouth of the

Mississipi. **On page 69** it states that "**the company of India**

had a trading post at Juda (Gulf of Benin) there it competed with all the nations of Europe! The **Portuguese was taking the upper hand at Juda**!

The French took their slaves from the Kingdom of Judah and landed them in the mouth of the Mississipi River. This means that if your family (Afrian American) can draw its lineage back to the state of Mississipi you are definitely from the tribe of Judah! The French also colonized Louisiana, Arkansas, Mississipi, Detroit, Texas, Florida Alabama and Saint Louis! Take your time and think about what I am about to say, do you remember when I showed you that the Bantu language was indeed the hebrew language? There is a book called the African heritage of american english, authored by Joseph e. holloway that lists Bantu (Hebrew) place names in the south. Lets see if this matches the Judaen captives brought to North America by the French. Bantu (Hebrew) place names were found in; Mississisipi, Louisiana and Alabama. There is another thing that one must never forget, it is written that Judah and Levi must dwell together and so we have the tribe of Judah and the Ashanti here in the United States of America. There was recorded two great migrations of the so called Negro from the south to Chicago, Newyork, Detroit, Washington , Milwaukee, Philadelphia,California, and so Judah and Levi is in the hood! Don't forget that the first great black migration was the Bantu migration of the black Hebrew Israelites to West Africa.

CHAPTER 13   BRITISH/ AMERICAN/ COLONIES

It is a known fact historically that there was a tribe of people called the Ashanti who controlled the Gold Coast of West Africa.

ASHANTI LEVIT E PRIEST

137

The Ashanti were acknowledged to be the tribe of Levi by the London Times and The Queen of England. The Ashanti was situated next to the tribe of Judah on the west coast of Africa and according to the historians they defeated the British Empire in three out of 4 wars. They were a great and noble Kingdom that refused to be dominated by the British even to the point of death. Their resistance to the British labeled them as being mean and rebellious, what would you do if your country or empire was being invaded by aliens? There refusal to be enslaved created one slave market for them and that market was the British colonies! The west african captives were taken from Whyday or the Kingdom of Judah, Ashanti/ Levite, Gold Coast, Slave Coast, Guinea, Congo and Angola. These captives went into the British colonies in Belize, Jamaica , Cayman Islands, Virgin Islands Barbados, Grenada and North America.

HEBREWS IN BRITISH CENTRAL AMERICA

BELIZE

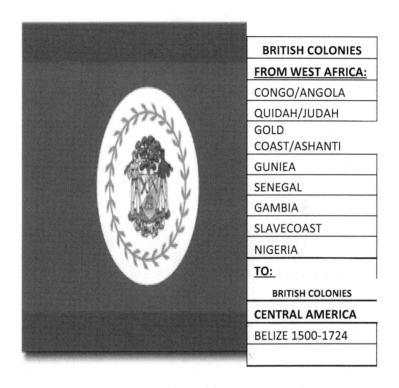

BRITISH COLONIES
FROM WEST AFRICA:
CONGO/ANGOLA
QUIDAH/JUDAH
GOLD COAST/ASHANTI
GUNIEA
SENEGAL
GAMBIA
SLAVECOAST
NIGERIA
TO:
BRITISH COLONIES
CENTRAL AMERICA
BELIZE 1500-1724

The West African speaking people of Belize are the seed of
the captives that the British (English) placed there. The people
in Belize are none other than the seed of the Kingdom of
Judah/Quidah/Whydah or Abier. Judah and Levi(Ashanti) are
right there in Belize and they don't even know who they are
that's why the Lord had it written in the scriptures that this is a
people robbed and spoiled (Isaiah 42:22), robbed

and spoiled of what? Your identity, the education that you receive is designed to keep you in the dark concerning the facts. It is a prescription for stupidity, it is designed to maintain your amnesia, to make you sleep with your eyes wide open! In the 43rd chapter of Isaiah the first verse it reads," But now thus says the Lord that created thee, o Jacob and he that formed thee o Israel fear not, for I have redeemed thee, I have called thee by they name, thou art mine! You brothers and sisters in Belize belong to the Lord God of Israel the God of Israel is your inheritance along with other things that I shall discuss with you later. In Isaiah 49:15 it is written." Can a woman forget her suckling child, that she should not have compassion on the son of her womb? Yea they may forget, yet will I not forget thee. Verse 17 behold, I have graven thee upon the palms of of my hands; thy walls are continually before me! Your God is calling you to wake up out of your deep sleep and call on him, for his arrival to the earth is soon to come.

What more can I say about these West African Hebrews? It was reported that the Ashanti circumcised their sons on the 8th day and kept the Saturday Sabbath days. Examine the Papal Bulls that the Pope issued concerning the slave trade and the letter that the Queen of the Ashanti sent to the Queen of England concerning the Sabbath.

PAPAL BULL-POPE NICHOLAS THE V

ROMAN PONTIFEX

The Roman Pontific issued by Pope Nicholas v sanctioned the seizure of non Christian lands and encouraged the enslavement of non Christian people in Africa. See the Negro Question part 1, pages 56, 57 and 58, the Author; Lee Cummings....that's me.

COUNCIL OF LAODOCEA

Christians must not Judaize by resting on the Sabbath day but must work on that day, rather honoring the Lords day (Sunday) if they be found resting as Christians on Saturday let them be anathema from Christ!

THE LETTER

We hear that her law (The Queen of England) is not so, nevertheless we have great joy in sending her our (The Ashanti/Levites) congratulations and we pray the great God Nyankopon on whom men lean and do not fall whose day of worship is Saturday!

So then who were the non-Christians on the coast of West Africa? It was the Ashanti Empire with its Levite priests and the brothers from the Kingdom of Judah. They were the ones who kept the Sabbath day and they were the ones whose lands were confiscated, and sold into the North Atlantic slave trade. These facts are indisputable and the question that you should be asking is what does all of this mean? Do the math, the West Africans lost their freedom and land from Senegal, Gambia,

Sierre Leonne, Windward Coast, Tooth Coast, Gold Coast, Kingdom of Judah, Nigeria, **Guinea**, Congo, Angola to South Africa. These were the People that the Popes in Europe despised because they worshipped the God of the bible, fact not fiction! If you are the seed of the West African captive in South America, Central America , British Central America, British Jamaica, British Cayman Islands, British Virgin Islands, British Barbados, British Grenada and British North America (America) you are the children of the Empire (Ashanti Empire) and you are indeed the children of the Kingdom of Judah.

TO THE HEBREWS IN BRITISH NORTH AMERICA

There are so many Hebrews in the past from America that I would be all day mentioning the heroics of each one so instead, I decided to create a wall of fame. If I were to write about the exploits of Martin Luther King, Harriet Tubman, Marcus Garvey, Nat Turner, Paul Cuffy, W.E.B Dubois, George Washington Carver, Malcom X, Jesse Jackson and Obama, I would never ever get to the end of this book. There is only one athlete that should have made this wall of fame in my mind and that would have been the boxer, Muhummad

Ali!

LEE CUMMINGS WALL OF FAME: NORTH AMERICA

| Nat Turner | PAUL CUFFY | MARCUS GARVEY |

| MARTIN L KING | MALCOLM X | OBAMA |

| W.E.B DUBOIS | GEORGE CARVER | JESSE JACKSON |

HARRIET TUBMAN SOJOURNER TRUTH FREDERICK DOUGLAS

I know that there are probably going to be someone who you thought should have made my hall of fame but I really didn't have the room to include any more of our people. All of these men but Obama have something in common they all are the descendants of our fathers who were brought to America by the British. It can never be overstated or understated that the British had a Factory at (Guinea) Judah just like the other European powers of that day. The British was in steady conflict with the West African Empire of the Ashanti and when the British won they transported the Ashanti to their colonies in Belize, Jamaica, and the Americas! There was a prophecy in the book of Genesis (Genesis 49:10) that the scepter shall not depart from Judah or the lawgiver from between his feet. The lawgiver is the Ashanti who had control of the gold coast and the

The scepter was in the hand of the Kingdom of Judah/Whydah per the map left to us by Emanuel Bowen 1747. There is a book called the Hebrewisms' of West Africa on page 17, it states," that the British took their captives from the Gold Coast/Ashanti/Levite and the French and the Spanish took their captives from Whydah/Slave Coast/Judah". **It appears that the tribe of Judah went into the Americas' first to be followed by the tribe of Levi!** The French brought Judah into the captivity see below.

LOUISIANA STATE UNIVERSITY
THE SHIPS THAT CAME FROM JUDAH

There is a publication written at Louisiana state University
　Titled: Creole New Orleans
　Race and Americanization
　Edited by R. Hirsch and Joseph Logsdon
　Louisiana State University Press
　Baton Rouge and London

On page 67 of this publication are the notes of a white slaver recalling the inventory of human beings on a cargo ship.....lets' see what he writes. He writes that " sixteen slave trading ships arrived from the Senegal region. **Six ships came**

from Juda and landed at the mouth of the Mississipi and in 1731 one ship form **juda** landed 464 slaves at the mouth of the Mississipi. Judah was dropped off in Mississipi & Louisiana.

CHAPTER 14   PORTUGUESE SOUTH AMERICAN

COLONY

BRAZIL

**Figure 67 EDSON ARANTES DO NASCIMENTO/ PELE
BETTER KNOW AS PELE; THE GREATEST SOCCER
PLAYER THAT THE WORLD HAS EVER SEEN.**

These West Africans in Brazil were dropped off by the Portuguese who captured and purchased them from the Kingdom of

147

Judah on the coast of West Africa. This is indisputable for it is widely known by the elite in high places that when the Portuguese arrived in Quidah/Judah, there was a town there called Ajuda. It is also known that the fort the Portuguese constructed in the Kingdom of Judah/slave coast was called to this day fort Ajuda!

THE DOOR OF NO RETURN

This is the door (gateway) that the children of Judah/ Brazil had to pass thru to be loaded on to the slave ships that would be waiting on the coast. In fact President Obama and his wife Michelle just visited fort Ajudah in July of 2013. The thing that I found to be interesting about their visit was that the Associated press nor any of the international news outlets mentioned that this was indeed fort Ajudah, now why would that be? In fact, neither the President nor his wife made mention of the town called neither Ajudah nor the name of the fort Ajudah! That's something for you to chew on but lets' continue with Brazil. And so it was that the sons of Judah came into the Brazilian captivity by the hands of the kidnapper Christopher Columbus (Colon). It was said that Brazil was the richest colony in the Americas because of the sugar plantations.

DUTCH SOUTH AMERICAN COLONIES

GUYANA

**Figure 68 THIS IS A STATUE OF CUFFY; HE LED A
SUCCESSFUL SLAVE UPRISING IN BERBICE GUYANA**

Life is interesting to say the least, you go thru life thinking that you are wise and that you have arrived but God continues to show you new things and it humbles you. I had never heard of Cuffy until I set out to do the sequel to the Negro Question. Yet history knows him as a hero, the man who led a 2500 man slave (captive) revolt against the white colonizers. He eventually became governor of Guyana but as usual a civil war broke out among the sons of Judah and Cuffy after losing, killed himself....what a shame.

DUTCH COLONIES IN AMERICA

The Africans of the East coast of America have their

origins in Senegal, Gambia, Windward Coast, the Gold

Coast/Ashanti/ Levites, Slave Coast/Kingdom of

Judah/Savi/Whydah/Quidah/Congo/ Guinea and Angola. Your accent can be explained by the fact that the Dutch was the first European power to colonize America. You accent is Part Dutch and part English. I don't need to write to you because the word of the Lord is with you brothers and sisters in New York and New Jersey. We can see your light from as far as Chicago…..that's a pretty bright light. I find fault with you brothers because of the rage by which you kill one another. I find fault with the abortion rate among the sisters on the east coast. It has been said that for every Negro child that is born that two children are aborted. I have a huge problem with this number. I have a problem with the entire afro-American captivity and that is the fact that we abort 550,000 black babies in the womb every year. This is an abomination in the eyes of the living God for it is written; "slay not the innocent for I will not hold him guiltless that doeth such" what is more innocent than an unborn child?

THE CONSPIRATORS:

I have decided to give you a list of the nations, churches, museums, Kings, Universities and Newspapers who have known for hundreds of years who you are.

THE ROMAN CATHOLIC CHURCH

TWO PAPAL BULLS

Pope Nicholas 5th (Papacy 1447-1455)

Issued Papal bull: THE DUM DIVERSAS

POPE ALEXANDER THE V1

Issued Papal Bull: INTER CAETERA

THE KINGS OF EUROPE:

KING LOUIS 15TH OF FRANCE

KING EDWARD OF ENGLAND

THE EUROPEAN PRESS:

THE LONDON TIMES

THE AMERICAN UNIVERSITIES

BOSTON UNIVERSITY

LOUISIANA STATE UNIVERSITY

NORTHWESTERN UNIVERSITY

MUSEUMS

FRENCH MUSEUM, FRANCE

BRITISH MUESUM, LONDON

THE KINGS PRINCES AND DONS FOUND

ON SLAVE PLANTATIONS

1. BENKO BIOHO-AFRICAN KING OF

COLUMBIA-

SENEGAL, WIKIPEDIA ENCYCLOPEDIA

2. BONA FICIO PINEDO- SENEGAL/

BOLIVIAN KING

WIKIPEDIA ENCYCLOPEDIA

3. JULIO PINEDO- SENEGAL / BOLIVIAN

KING

WIKIPEDIA ENCYCLOPEDIA

4. GASPAR YANGA- GABON/MEXICAN KING

WIKIPEDIA ENCYCLOPEDIA

5. BAYANO – GHANA PRINCE/ PANAMANIAN KING

WIKIPEDIA ENCYCLOPEDIA

6. ABDUL RAHMAN IBRAHAM-PRINCE OF FULLANI/GUINEA, ABDUL FOUND ON PLANTATION IN MISSISIPI, NORTH AMERICA. WIKIPEDIA

7. TACKY-AFRICAN KING/CHIEF-, GHANA JAMAICA, WIKIPEDIA ENCYCLOPEDIA

8. KING JUNE –AKAMU CHIEF/ ST JOHNS INDIES

WIKIPEDIA ENCYCLOPEDIA

9. KING BOLOMBO-ADAMBE KING- ST JOHNS

WIKIPEDIA ENCYCLOPEDIA

10. PRINCE UKAWSAW GRONNIOSA-

BARBADOS FOUND IN NEWJERSEY

PLANTATION

WIKIPEDIA ENCYCLOPEDIA

11. PRINCE AQUASHI-AQUAMBO PRINCE,

ST JOHNS

WIKIPEDIA ENCYCLOPEDIA

12. PRINCE BREFU-?

13. PRINCE KANTU-?

14. PRINCE BROTEER FURO-BOURNOU

NEW JERSEY

15. PRINCE-L TOUSSAINT OVERTURE-

ARADA   BENIN, HAITI

WIKIPEDIA ENCYCLOPEDIA

16. PRINCE CRISPUS ATTUCKS/

GUINEA/BENIN

BOSTON TEA PARTY

17. PRINCE- OLAUDAH EQUIANO-?

3 DONS?

CONCLUSION

My conclusion will be the dialogue between two White

men, (Doug and Bob) discussing the black mans situation in

the Americas and Caribbean.

(DOUG)

The Negro must never know the truth about the empire that

he came from. He must never know that his fathers were

empire builders, that he had the first Universities and that he

wrote and spoke Hebrew. In order to do this we will have to

destroy his libraries, pictures and burn his books. Yes....and

then...then.... we will have to fill in the gaps with our own

made up history. We will pass laws making it illegal for the

Negro not to attend one of our free institutions (Public School)

daily and if he refuses to show up for a false education we will fine his parents and incarcerate them. From the time that his children have the ability to reason we will plant the seeds of white history on the front lobes of his mind. We will search out and find the smartest and wittiest of them to indoctrinate in our Universities and send them back to the black community with our lies. The education will be regulated by the government and he will be forced to teach what we tell him to teach…nothing more and nothing less.

(BOB)

Won't his black leaders and teachers alert him to our lies?

(DOUG)

His black leaders? We will choose his leaders for him and with the education that he will receive in our Universities he will not only teach our lies but he will defend our version of the truth to the death and he will be just like a rat taking poison back to the nest. The Negro leader will be the instrument by which we will indoctrinate the Negro all over the Americas and the Caribbean.

(BOB)

I see......they would never believe the lie if it came from a white man so it makes sense to send their own black leaders to do our dirty work!

(DOUG)

Wow the light bulb has finally gone off in your mind.

(BOB)

What about the artifacts, images and ancient documents dug up by the archaeologist that will prove that what we are teaching lies?

(DOUG)

That's simple, we will use the power of silence to discredit them or we can simply ignore them. If that fails we will tell the Negro community that they are an occult!

DOUGS' SMILE HAS BEEN REPLACED BY SADNESS

(BOB)

Why have you become so sad Doug?

(DOUG)

I fear that the worst mistake that we as white people have made is the invention of the internet. With this invention the Negro will no longer have to rely on a free public education. He now has the ability to go on line and research everything that he was ever taught. At some point he won't need to rely on the black teachers that we indoctrinate. The Negro can research the libraries of every nation on the earth from his living room, he will be able to investigate every important archaeological find and this could prove fatal in our brainwash of him and his children.

I have written this with my own hands

BROTHER LEE CUMMINGS!

REFERENCES:

<u>MAPS:</u>

THE KINGDOM OF JUDAH- EMANUEL BOWEN
NORTHWESTERN LIBRARY, PAGE-4

HERODUTUS MAP OF THE WORLD PAGE-51 WIKIPEDIA

BANTU MIGRATION, PAGES 55, 57 & 58 TIME LINE MAPS

TARIM BASIN XIANG CHINA, PAGE-63 WIKIPEDIA

GABON WEST AFRICA, PAGE 109 WIKIPEDIA

ASHANTI KINGDOM, PAGE-126,132 WIKIPEDIA

HEBREW IMAGES TAKEN FROM BLACK OBELISK

BLACK ASSYRIAN OBELISK, PAGE 18-BRITISH MUSEUM

HEBREW PROCESSION PAGES 18-21-BRITISH MUSEUM

HEBREW IMAGES TAKEN FROM SENNACHERIBS PRISM

2 CORN ROLLED HEBREW ISRAELITES PAGES 22-27-BRITISH MUSEUM

HEBREW IMAGES TAKEN FROM ASSYRIAN RELIEF NIMRUD

NAPHTALI GOING INTO CAPTIVITY, PAGES 28-30-BRITISH MUSEUM.

IMAGE OF MANSA MUSA PAGE 56-WIKIPEDIAN ENCYCLOPEDIA

TARIM MUMMIES PAGE 62-WIKIPEDIA ENCYCLOPEDIA

BIBLE LONG COUNT PAGE 64- THE BIBLE

ANKROTIRI FRESCO THE SHIP PROCESSION PAGE 65, 66, &67 WIKIPEDIA

BLACK ROMAN POET, VIRGIL PAGE 70, BARDO MUSEUM, TUNIS TUNISIA

ROMAN CITIZEN PAGE 71, BACCANTI TARQUINIA

GHENGIS KHAN PAGE 72- NATIONAL TAPEI MUSEUM KUBLAI KHAN PAGE 73-TAPEI MUSEUM

GERMAN TAPESTRY PG 74-MOORISH HISTORY, DAISHIKI JONES

BLACK KINGS AND POPES

RUSSIAN KING MIRIAN 3 PAGE 75-SVETITSKHOVELI CATHEDRAL GEORGIA RUSSIA

HUNGARIAN KING BELA PAGE 76-NATIONAL LIBRARY, BUDAPAST

KING ALEXIS 1 PAGE 76- VATICAN LIBRARY

KING CHARLES 5TH KING OF FRANCE PAGE 81& 82- LARCO MUSEUM LIMA PERU

BLACK AVIGNON POPES PAGE 77- PAINTING DONE BY
GIOVANNI DI PAOLO 1460

BLACK KING LEOPOLD PAGE 78 & 79 – MACKUBURG
CATHEDRAL

MARIA THERESA HABSBURG 80-MACKUBURG
CATHEDRAL

CHARLEMAGNE KING OF FRANKS PAGE 83-
KARTSTEJN CASTLE CZECH REPUBLIC

KING FREDERICK 1 BARBOSSA PAGE 84- MUSEUM
CORRER VENICE

ICONS OF BRITISH AND IRISH SAINTS PAGES 86&87-
EASTERN ORTHODOX CHURCH SAINT SERAPHIM CHURCH
WALSINGHAM, NORFOLK ENGLAND

BLACK KNIGHT OF EUROPE PAGE 88-WIENER
NEUSTADT ABBEY SEFANSDAM VIENNA

BLACK KNIGHT PAGE 89, MAGDEBURG CATHEDRAL
BENJAMIN FRANKLINS LETTER

STATUE OF A BLACK MOOR KNIGHT PAGE 90-
MAGDEBURG CATHEDRAL

KING EDWARD 2 OF ENGLAND PAGE 95- GEORGE
CHAPEL, WINDSOR

KING GEORGE 3RD PAGE 96- DICTIONARY OF
NATIONAL BIOGRAPHY, STEPHEN LESLIE ORIG
PUBLICATION 1885-1900

QUEEN CHARLOTTE PAGE 97, DICTIONARY OF NATIONAL BIOGRAPHY, STEPHEN LESLIE ORIG PUBLICATION 1885-1900

ASHANTI PRIEST CROSSING PRAH RIVER PAGE 101- THE NEGRO QUESTION PT 1 PAGE24

JOSE LEONARDO CHIRINO VENEZUELA PAGE 102 AFRO VENEZUELA.COM

BENKO BIOHO PAGE 103- AFRO COLOMBIA.COM

ALONSO DE ILLESCAS EUCADOR PAGE 104- AFRO ECUADOR.COM

3DONS PAGE 104- LARCO MUSEUM, LIMA PERU

MARI ELENA MOYANA PAGE 105-PERU/ WIKIPEDIA

JEAN BEAUSJOUR PAGE 105 CHILE/ WIKIPEDIA

FIDEL NADA PAGE 106/ ARGENTINA WIKIPEDIA

NOELIA MACIEL PAGE 106 URUGAY WIKIPEDIA

KING BONIFICIO PAGE 107 BOLIVIA, AFRO BOLIVIA.COM

KING JULIO PINEDO PAGE- 107, AFRO BOLIVIA.COM

YANGA PRINCE OF GABON, PAGE 109-MEXICO AFRO MEXICO.COM

BLACK POWER FIST PAGE 110 WIKIPEDIA

IMAGES OF BLACK ARABS

CREDITS TO THE BROTHERS WHO DONATED MONEY FOR THE PRINTING OF THIS BOOK

AZARIAH ISRAEL/ CHICAGO ILLINOIS
JOSHUA LEVITE/ ILLINOIS
MICHAEL ISRAEL/ ATLANTA GEORGIA